Vacation Destination Travel Guide To

OBAN,

SCOTLAND

The Must-Have Travel Companion to the
Enchanting City of Oban

Curtis Chase

COPYRIGHT NOTICE

DISCLAIMER

Please note that the information contained within this document is for educational purposes only. The information contained herein has been obtained from sources believed to be reliable at the time of publication. The opinions expressed herein are subject to change without notice.

Readers acknowledge that the Author / Publisher is not engaging in rendering legal, financial or professional advice. The Publisher / Author disclaims all warranties as to the accuracy, completeness, or adequacy of such information.

The Publisher assumes no liability for errors, omissions, or inadequacies in the information contained herein or from the interpretations thereof. The publisher / Author specifically disclaims any liability from the use or application of the information contained herein or from the interpretations thereof.

TABLE OF CONTENTS

INTRODUCTION

WELCOME TO OBAN!

Tucked down on Scotland's west coast, Oban is well known for its breathtaking landscape, fascinating past, and lively culture. Every visitor may find something to love in Oban, whether it be its charming harbor, its historical sites, or its mouthwatering seafood meals.

Oban...With Open Arms

Beautiful hillsides and craggy coasts will surround you as you travel to Oban. With kind residents, quaint bars, and a laid-back pace of life, the town itself radiates warmth.

Being the entry point to the Inner Hebrides, Oban's busy harbour is a well-liked destination for island hopping and seeing the breathtaking islands of Staffa, Iona and Mull. But Oban is a destination unto itself, full of sights, activities, and experiences just waiting to be explored. It's more than just a starting place for island excursions.

About This Travel Guide

Your indispensable travel companion for seeing Oban and its environs is this handbook. Enriched with insider knowledge, thorough details, and useful guidance, this book is meant to help you make the most of your stay in Oban and guarantee a happy and unforgettable experience.

What This Handbook Includes

- Thorough examination of Oban's sights, icons, and undiscovered treasures.
- Local advice for eating, shopping, nightlife, and outdoor pursuits.
- Usable details on modes of transportation, lodging choices, and safety precautions.

- Historical context, cultural observations, and local manners advice to improve your knowledge and enjoyment of Oban.
- Sample itineraries and recommendations to help you make the most of your time and make priceless memories.

This book offers all you need to plan the ideal vacation to Oban and maximize your Scottish adventure, regardless of your level of experience.

Why Oban?

You might be asking yourself, "Why Oban?" for your next vacation. Your bucket list should include Oban for the following reasons, just a few:

Stunning Scenery: From peaceful lochs to soaring mountains, Oban is encircled by some of Scotland's most spectacular scenery. Particularly around dusk, the views of the port and the neighboring islands are utterly captivating.

Rich History: Oban is replete with history and legacy, having ancient origins.

Discover more about the town's intriguing past by touring historic sites including McCaig's Tower, Dunollie Castle, and the Oban War and Peace Museum.

Culinary Delights: Foodies will love Oban for its fresh seafood, locally grown vegetables, and classic Scottish cuisine. Savor locally made black pudding and haggis, indulge in freshly caught fish and chips, and don't pass up the opportunity to tour the Oban Distillery and try some of its well-known whisky.

Outdoor Adventures: Oban has a plethora of outdoor pursuits to suit every interest, whether you're an adrenaline junkie or a naturalist. Adventures abound in and around Oban, from boat trips and animal viewing to hiking and kayaking.

Warm Hospitality: Greetings from the people are one of the pleasures of visiting Oban. The inhabitants of Oban, who are renowned for their friendliness and hospitality, are always delighted to share their enthusiasm for their town and provide insider advice to help you make the most of your visit.

How To Use This Guide

Although getting about a new place can be intimidating, this guide is here to assist!

Here's how to maximize this travel manual:

Navigation: To quickly go between chapters and get the information you need, use the table of contents. Whether creating an itinerary, looking for places to eat, or looking for helpful advice, everything is arranged for convenience.

Insider Tips: Watch out for insider advice and suggestions throughout the book. Make the most of your time in Oban by learning from residents and seasoned tourists about hidden treasures and avoiding tourist traps.

Practical Information: Read the sections on transportation, lodging, safety advice, and other pertinent information. These pointers will guarantee a seamless and trouble-free trip whether you're organizing your itinerary or negotiating Oban's streets.

Sample Itineraries: Use these suggested schedules and sample itineraries to help you arrange your stay in Oban.

Whether you're coming for a weekend escape, an outdoor adventure, or a cultural immersion, these itineraries offer ideas and direction for planning your own amazing trip.

With these pointers and the tools in this book, you'll be prepared to confidently explore Oban, fully experience its history and culture, and make priceless memories of your Scottish vacation.

CHAPTER 1

INTRODUCTION TO OBAN

On Scotland's west coast sits the charming seaside town of Oban, sometimes known as the "Gateway to the Isles." Travelers looking for adventure, relaxation, and discovery now flock to Oban because of its breathtaking natural beauty, rich history, and lively culture.

We shall give a summary of Oban in this chapter, go into its interesting past, examine its topography and climate, and reveal its own customs and culture.

Overview Of Oban

Overlooking the Firth of Lorn, Oban is a town in the Scottish Argyll and Bute. Being the biggest town in the region, it is a vital center for transportation that links the Inner Hebrides islands to mainland Scotland. Oban, for all its modest size, has a busy harbor, quaint alleys dotted with cafes and stores, and stunning views of the surrounding coastline.

Tourists swarm to Oban to see its ancient sites, enjoy its famous seafood cuisine, and go on excursions to other islands and attractions, which drives the town's economy mostly. From history aficionados to foodies, Oban has much to offer every kind of traveler.

History Of Oban

Oban has thousands of years of history, with Mesolithic era human habitation documented in the region. But the town as we know it now started to take shape in the eighteenth century, when its advantageous position on Scotland's west coast made it a major hub for trade and business.

Arriving of the railway in the middle of the 19th century, which made Oban a well-liked tourist destination, was one of the most important events in its history. Hotels, guesthouses and other tourist facilities sprang up in Oban as a result of the influx of tourists from Glasgow and beyond who came to appreciate its natural beauty and beachside attractions.

Oban had through a prosperous and expanding time in the Victorian era when famous sites like McCaig's Tower, a towering coliseum-style building that overlooks the town, were built. Oban offers tourists an intriguing window into its past with its museums, architectural style, and cultural legacy.

Geography And Climate

Blessed with a varied terrain, Oban is home to stunning islands, undulating hills, and craggy coasts. The village is encircled by breathtakingly beautiful landscape, which is dramatically framed by the seaside peaks of Ben Lui and Ben Cruachan.

Oban's seaside location has an impact on its climate, which is year-round warm with little rain. With their usually warm and sunny weather, summers are the best season to discover outdoor sights and engage in sports like hiking, kayaking, and wildlife observation.

Though the winters are colder, Oban is a nice place to visit all year round because it seldom gets too cold or snowed.

Culture And Traditions

Oban's nautical past, close-knit community spirit, and Gaelic origins have all influenced its rich cultural legacy. Place names, traditional music, and cultural events such the yearly Highland Games and the Oban Live Music Festival all bear witness to the town's Gaelic past.

A centuries-old athletic competition featuring traditional Scottish sports including caber tossing, hammer throwing, and Highland dancing, the Highland Games are one of Oban's most treasured customs. An international draw for athletes and spectators, the games represent a high point of the town's cultural calendar.

Additionally, well-known for its thriving music culture are live concerts held all year long in bars, restaurants, and concert halls in Oban. Every taste in music is catered to in Oban, from modern rock and pop to traditional folk music.

Along with its cultural activities and customs, Oban is well-known for its seafood dishes, which are made using fresh fish and shellfish that are gathered every day from the Firth of Lorn. At eateries and seafood shacks all throughout town, visitors can try regional specialties such oysters from Oban Bay, scallops from the West Coast, and just caught langoustines.

Oban is a warm and lively place for visitors from near and far because, all things considered, its culture and customs reflect its rich history, stunning surroundings, and strong feeling of community.

CHAPTER 2

PLANNING YOUR TRIP

A journey to Oban needs careful thought given to a number of things, such as when is the best to go and how to get there and where to stay.

We will go over all you need to know to plan your trip to Oban and enjoy your stay in this little seaside town in this chapter.

Best Time To Visit

Your tastes and interests will determine when is the best to visit Oban because the town has something special to offer all year long. The several seasons are broken out here, along with what to anticipate in each:

Spring (March To May): Oban is a wonderful place to come in the spring when the surroundings are a riot of vibrant flowers and lush vegetation. Walking, animal viewing, and touring the town's attractions are all made much easier by the usually pleasant weather. Because spring also heralds in the start of the tourist season, you may anticipate less people and cheaper lodging costs than during the busiest summer months.

Summer (June To August): With its pleasant weather, long days, and packed schedule of events and activities, summer is the busiest season in Oban. An great time to visit the town is when it comes alive with festivals, outdoor concerts, and cultural activities. Still, expect more people and more expensive costs—especially for lodging and excursions. Booking your lodging and activities early in advance will help you to guarantee your desired dates.

Autumn (September To November): Oban is best seen in the fall when the surrounding countryside becomes a magnificent tapestry of crimson, orange, and gold. Walking, biking, and scenic drives are all excellent outdoor activities during this still-relatively-warm season. Harvest festivals and culinary events in the town during the fall provide another chance to try seasonal fare and locally grown vegetables.

Winter (December To February): Although less crowded than the busiest travel season, winter in Oban has its own special appeals. Even if the weather is colder, the town becomes cozier with holiday décor, roaring fires, and kind people. The winter is a great time to visit indoor sites such galleries, museums, and whisky distilleries and to eat substantial Scottish comfort food in neighborhood bars and restaurants.

Your interests and tastes will ultimately determine when is the ideal time to visit Oban. Oban offers year-round outdoor adventures, cultural encounters, or just a peaceful retreat.

How To Get To Oban

Oban is conveniently reachable by a number of transportation options, including:

By Car: From Glasgow or Edinburgh, driving is the most practical method to get to Oban. Depending on the traffic and state of the roads, the trip from Glasgow takes two to three hours and from Edinburgh three to four hours.

The principal roads to Oban, the A82 and A85, provide picturesque drives through the Scottish countryside.

By Train: Oban is also reachable by train from Glasgow Queen Street Station. Regular services by ScotRail travel to Oban in about three hours and thirty minutes. Said to be one of the most picturesque rail routes in the nation, the trip provides breathtaking vistas of the Scottish Highlands.

By Bus: From major cities and towns in Scotland, a number of bus companies run trips to Oban. Daily departures of Citylink's direct bus services from Glasgow and Edinburgh to Oban are many. Bus travel takes around three to four hours from Glasgow and four to five hours from Edinburgh.

By Ferry: Caledonian MacBrayne (CalMac) runs ferries to Oban for visitors arriving from the Inner Hebrides islands or other coastal towns. Being in the town center, the ferry terminal makes it simple to get to Oban's facilities and attractions after arrival.

By Air: Although Oban lacks an airport of its own, Glasgow and Edinburgh airports are the closest and provide both domestic and international travel.

You can get to Oban by private transfer, train or bus, or vehicle rental from the airports.

Getting Around Oban

It's simple and practical to navigate about Oban once you're here. Because the town center is walkable and comparatively small, it's perfect for leisurely strolls and self-guided tours. Here are other choices, though, if you would rather take public transportation or must go greater distances:

Walking: Oban has sidewalks, crosswalks, and roadways designed for pedestrians in its town center. Walking distance separates a lot of the town's attractions, stores, eateries, and lodgings, so you can see Oban at your own speed and enjoy its sights and sounds.

Local Buses: In and around Oban, West Coast Motors runs local bus services that link to neighboring towns, tourist destinations, and picturesque locations. With so many bus stops around the area and reasonably priced tickets, it's a practical way to travel about.

Taxis: You may book ahead of time or hail a taxi on the street in Oban.

In the town centre and close to the train and ferry terminals are taxi ranks. Short travels or when you have to go outside of the town center make taxis a practical choice.

Car Rentals: Renting a car is a practical choice if you intend to explore the neighbourhood or go farther away. Numerous auto rental companies with facilities in Oban provide a selection of cars to fit your requirements and budget. Your own car enables you to go at your own speed and reach far-off places that might not be accessible by public transit.

Riding: With picturesque routes and trails open to cyclists of all skill levels, riding is a popular method to see Oban and the surrounding area. You can hire a bike in town or bring your own.

Accommodation Selections

Luxury hotels and quaint guesthouses to bed & breakfasts and self-catering apartments are just a few of the lodging choices available in Oban to fit every taste and budget. Following are a few lodging choices in Oban:

Hotels: Oban is home to a number of hotels, from opulent facilities with views of the water to reasonably priced choices in the town centre. There are many different possibilities available, whether your tastes run to a family-friendly resort with on-site facilities or a chic boutique hotel.

Bed And Breakfasts And Guesthouses: Think about staying at an Oban bed and breakfast or guesthouse for a more individualized and personal experience. Often, kind hosts who may offer advice and insider knowledge for seeing the region oversee these little lodgings.

Self-Catering Apartments: These are a terrific choice if you would like more freedom and flexibility while you are here. The kitchens or kitchenettes in these fully furnished apartments let you cook for yourself and have a home-away-from-home experience in Oban.

Hostels: Those on a tight budget might find reasonably priced lodging choices in shared dorm-style rooms with shared amenities. A terrific place to meet other tourists and trade advice and suggestions for seeing Oban and beyond is at a hostel.

Campsites And Caravan Parks: Oban and the neighbouring areas provide a range of camping and RV parks for those looking for a more outdoor experience.

There are campsites with contemporary amenities and stunning natural surrounds whether you'd rather set up a tent beneath the stars or park your trailer or motorhome in a picturesque spot.

Selecting Your Ideal Accommodation

Your tastes, spending limit, and mode of travel should all be taken into account while choosing lodging in Oban. To remember are the following:

Location: Choose between a more remote area outside of town, the harbor, or the core of the town. When selecting your lodging, think about how close you are to restaurants, sights, and modes of transportation.

Amenities: Think about what features—such free Wi-Fi, parking, onsite dining, or recreational activities like spas or swimming pools—are most important to you. Select lodging that provides the conveniences and extras that will make your time in Oban more enjoyable.

Budget: Decide on a spending limit for your lodging and search for possibilities that are within it.

Though costs may change throughout the year, try to be flexible with your vacation dates.

Reviews And Ratings: To have a sense of the general caliber and experience of the lodging, check the reviews and ratings left by past visitors. Seek for lodgings with great ratings for cleanliness, comfort, and friendliness.

Packages And Special Offers: Watch for any packages, special offers, or discounts that could be accessible for the lodging of your choosing. Discounts are available at many hotels and guesthouses for earlier reservations, longer stays, or off-peak times of year.

Accessibility: When making your reservation, be sure to ask about accessibility amenities such wheelchair ramps, elevators, and accessible rooms if you have certain accessibility needs or mobility issues.

All things considered, selecting the proper lodging is a crucial part of organizing your visit to Oban and can have a big effect on how you feel there overall. Oban has many different choices to meet the needs and tastes of any traveler, whether you want opulent lodging with breathtaking views or quaint guesthouses with a personal touch.

CHAPTER 3

ACCOMODATION IN OBAN

Selecting the appropriate lodging when organizing your visit to Oban is essential to making sure your stay is pleasurably comfortable.

Oban provides a wide variety of lodging choices to meet the demands and tastes of every visitor, ranging from opulent resorts to quaint bed and breakfasts.

This chapter will go into the different kinds of lodging options in Oban and offer advice on how to select the ideal location to stay while there.

General Overview Of Accommodation Choices

Oban provides a large variety of lodging choices to suit all tastes, budgets, and vacation patterns.

Oban offers a wide range of lodging options, from opulent hotels with breath-taking vistas to charming guesthouses with individualized care and inexpensive hostels for a stay that won't break the bank.

The various forms of lodging are summarized here:

Hotels: Oban has a number of hotels, from upmarket places with views of the water to more affordable choices in the town center. With so many facilities, such as fitness centers, concierge services, and on-site dining, hotels are perfect for anyone looking for ease and comfort.

Guesthouses and Bed & Breakfasts: If you're looking for a more individualized and small-scale experience, think about staying in an Oban guesthouse. Often, kind hosts who may offer advice and insider knowledge for seeing the region oversee these little lodgings.

Cozy rooms, homemade breakfasts, and a cordial Scottish welcome are all available to guests.

Self-Catering Apartments: Those looking for freedom and flexibility during their visit often choose self-catering apartments. With kitchens or kitchenettes, these completely furnished apartments let visitors cook for themselves and have a home-away-from-home experience in Oban. Family, group, or extended term visitors will find self-catering apartments to be perfect.

Hostels: In Oban, travelers on a tight budget will discover reasonably priced places to stay. For people who would want more solitude, hostels have private rooms in addition to dorm-style accommodations with communal amenities. Meeting other tourists and trading opinions and advice for seeing Oban and beyond is made easy in hostels.

Campsites And Caravan Parks: Outdoor enthusiasts will find a range of campsites and caravan parks in Oban and the surrounding areas. You'll find campsites with contemporary amenities and stunning natural surrounds whether you'd rather park your caravan in a picturesque spot or pitch a tent beneath the stars.

One excellent approach to enjoy outdoor pursuits like hiking, fishing, and animal viewing is to go camping.

Whatever your tastes or budget, Oban provides lodging choices to meet every requirement and guarantee a special stay in this quaint seaside town.

Luxury Resorts

Luxury resorts in Oban provide unmatched facilities, breathtaking vistas, and first-rate service to visitors looking for the height of comfort.

Top luxury resorts in Oban include the following:

The Manor House Hotel: Offering opulent lodging, excellent cuisine, and a variety of recreational amenities, The Manor House Hotel is tucked away among verdant grounds with a view of Oban Bay. The hotel's award-winning restaurant serves modern cuisine, and guests may unwind at the spa and wellness center or in roomy rooms and suites.

Perle Oban Hotel: Offering boutique rooms with modern decor and breathtaking harbour views, this hotel is situated in the middle of Oban.

The hotel offers opulently furnished rooms and suites, an onsite restaurant with regional fare, and a rooftop terrace with expansive views of the surroundings.

Isle Of Eriska Hotel: This private island off the coast of Oban provides a quiet haven encircled by breathtaking scenery. Private cottages strewn around the estate or tastefully appointed rooms and suites in the ancient main house are available for guests to stay. Along with a spa, golf course, Michelin-starred restaurant, and outdoor pursuits including hiking, fishing, and wildlife viewing, the hotel offers.

Airds Hotel and Restaurant: A short drive from Oban, in the charming village of Port Appin, lies the Airds Hotel and Restaurant, which provides opulent lodgings in a peaceful environment. Relax in uniquely styled rooms and suites, enjoy fine dining made with ingredients found locally, and take guided excursions and outdoor activities to discover the surrounding area.

Knipoch Hotel: Tucked away in acres of beautifully manicured grounds, this old country home provides a tranquil haven from the daily grind. Luxury lodging, authentic Scottish food, and friendly service are available to guests in a stunning location with a view of Loch Feochan.

These opulent Oban resorts offer the ideal fusion of style, coziness, and leisure, letting visitors take in the splendor of Scotland's west coast while savouring first-rate facilities and faultless service. These resorts in Oban provide a very remarkable experience whether you're looking for a quiet retreat, a family holiday, or a romantic escape.

Budget-Friendly Hotels

Budget-conscious visitors to Oban will find a variety of reasonably priced lodging choices, including hotels that provide convenience and comfort without going over budget.

For budget-conscious tourists hoping to see Oban and its environs without going over budget, these hotels offer basic conveniences and cozy lodgings at reasonable prices. Following are some reasonably priced hotels in Oban:

Oban Bay Hotel and Spa: This reasonably priced hotel has breathtaking views of Oban Bay and is situated on the waterfront promenade. The hotel has a spa with several treatments and therapies, a restaurant on site serving

Scottish food, and cozy rooms with contemporary conveniences.

The town centre, the ferry terminal, and the surrounding attractions are all conveniently close for visitors.

Regent Hotel: This handy location offers reasonably priced lodging in the city of Oban. Cozy rooms at the hotel provide flat-screen TVs, free Wi-Fi, and en suite bathrooms. The hotel's onsite restaurant and bar serves up classic pub meals and substantial Scottish breakfasts.

Columba Hotel: With expansive vistas of the harbor and the neighboring highlands, this reasonably priced hotel overlooks Oban Bay. The motel has cozy rooms with satellite TV, tea and coffee making supplies, and en suite bathrooms. Dining options include a range of Scottish and foreign cuisine at the hotel's restaurant, or unwind with a drink in the lounge bar.

Lancaster Hotel: This handy location offers reasonably priced lodgings within a short stroll from Oban's town center. Simple rooms at the hotel provide flat-screen TVs, free Wi-Fi, and en suite bathrooms. Every morning guests can unwind in the hotel's comfortable lounge area after a full Scottish breakfast.

St. Anne's Guest House: Tucked away in a residential neighborhood a short stroll from Oban's town centre, this quaint Victorian home provides reasonably priced lodging. Cozy rooms at the guest house provide flat-screen TVs, free Wi-Fi, and ensuite bathrooms. Every morning, visitors may have a filling breakfast in the dining room and take a leisurely stroll around the town.

Travelers looking for reasonably priced lodgings in this charming seaside town will find these inexpensive hotels in Oban to be the best value for their money. They offer cozy rooms and handy amenities.

Boutique Guesthouse

Boutique guesthouses in Oban provide distinctive lodgings with chic décor, excellent service, and a comfortable ambiance for those looking for a more private and individualized experience. Many times, these boutique hotels include specially decorated rooms, fine dining breakfasts, and other amenities that create an unforgettable experience. Oban has the following upscale guesthouses:

Roseneath Guest House: This charming Victorian mansion with a view of Oban Bay houses boutique lodgings with contemporary conveniences and tasteful décor.

Individually decorated rooms at the guest home have opulent furniture, Egyptian cotton sheets, and free toiletries. Each morning, visitors can unwind in the comfortable lounge area with expansive views of the bay or savour a delectable breakfast in the dining room.

Glenrigh Guest House: Offering boutique lodgings in a peaceful environment, Glenrigh Guest House is located in a quiet residential neighbourhood just a short stroll from Oban's town centre. Luxurious toiletries, soft bedding, and modern décor adorn the exquisitely furnished rooms of the guest home. Relax in the guest lounge or garden terrace after a freshly prepared breakfast using products acquired locally.

Braeside Guest House: Tucked away in the charming village of Connel, not far from Oban, Braeside Guest House provides upscale lodgings together with a cordial Scottish welcome. The guest house has quaint rooms furnished in period style, original artwork, and contemporary conveniences. Each morning, visitors can relax in the comfortable guest lounge with a choice of books, games, and DVDs or have a filling breakfast in the dining room.

Sutherland Guest House: Providing bespoke service and boutique lodgings with breathtaking views, Sutherland Guest House is situated in a peaceful residential neighbourhood overlooking Oban Bay. Individually designed rooms at the guest home have sumptuous bedding, plush bathrobes, and free drinks. The kind hosts will provide you expert advice and recommendations while you unwind in the guest lounge or garden patio and eat a wonderful breakfast every morning.

These Oban boutique guesthouses provide individualised care, chic lodgings, and meticulous attention to detail that will make your stay genuinely unforgettable. These boutique hotels in Oban offer the ideal environment for a laid-back vacation whether you're celebrating a particular occasion or just looking for a comfortable haven.

Unique Stays

Oban provides a range of distinctive lodgings that go beyond conventional hotels and guesthouses for those looking for a truly unique experience. These unusual lodgings, which range from quaint cottages and opulent glamping locations to old castles and lighthouses, offer a fascinating setting for your trip to Oban. Consider these unusual stays:

Barcaldine Castle: This medieval site offers a genuinely remarkable experience perched atop a hill overlooking Loch Creran. With breathtaking views of the surrounding countryside, four-poster beds, and exquisite chambers furnished in period, this renovated castle dates back to the 16th century. In addition to seeing the grounds and enjoying afternoon tea in the drawing room, guests can unwind by the fireplace in the great hall.

Easdale Island Bunkhouse: The Easdale Island Bunkhouse is a unique island retreat located on the peaceful island of Easdale. Simple lodgings in a former slate quarry building, this eco-friendly bunkhouse has shared kitchen facilities, dorm-style rooms, and expansive views of the surrounding sea and islands. Visitors can go boating to other islands, tour the Easdale Island Folk Museum, or explore the island's craggy shoreline.

Oban Bay Yurt: Perched atop a hillside with a view of Oban Bay, this is glamping done differently. This traditional Mongolian yurt has comfy furnishings, a private porch with amazing views, and a wood-burning stove for cozy lodgings. Through hikes in the neighboring forests, guests can take in the calm and quiet of the surrounding countryside, or they can stargaze from the outdoor hot tub.

Kilchurn Castle Lodge: On the banks of Loch Awe, this quaint lodge is situated only a short distance from the ancient Kilchurn Castle. This recently refurbished lodge provides cozy lodgings together with contemporary conveniences including a well-equipped kitchen, roomy sitting spaces, and outside lounging areas with views of the castle ruins. Visitors may stroll along the shoreline, fish on the loch, or see the castle grounds.

Kerrera Bunkhouse: For a tranquil haven encircled by nature, head to the remote island of Kerrera and stay at the Kerrera Bunkhouse. Simple lodgings in a renovated farm building, this environmentally friendly bunkhouse features shared kitchen facilities, dorm-style rooms, and breathtaking views of the surrounding countryside. Walking paths around the island, a visit to the ruins of Gylen Castle, or just unwinding in the peaceful surrounds are all available to visitors.

A genuinely unforgettable experience, these unusual accommodations in Oban let visitors fully enjoy the history, charm, and natural beauty of the Scottish countryside.

Accommodations Highly Recommended

Finding the ideal location to stay in Oban might be daunting because there are so many of lodging alternatives. Based on evaluations from guests, features, and general experience, here are some highly suggested lodgings in Oban to help you make your selections:

The Manor House Hotel: This hotel, which is located on the waterfront promenade, provides a variety of recreational activities together with tasteful eating and excellent lodging. Travelers laud the hotel's lovely setting, friendly staff, and cozy accommodations with breathtaking views of Oban Bay.

Roseneath Guest House: Offering stylishly decorated boutique rooms with contemporary conveniences, Roseneath Guest House overlooks Oban Bay. Warm welcome, mouthwatering meals, and expansive bay views are all highly praised by guests.

Oban Bay Hotel And Spa: This beachfront promenade hotel provides reasonably priced lodgings with breathtaking views of Oban Bay. Convenient location, amiable staff, and on-site spa amenities are valued by guests.

Perle Oban Hotel: Located in the centre of Oban, this boutique hotel has modern décor and expansive harbour views. The chic accommodations, first-rate restaurant, and rooftop terrace with a view of the town are all highly regarded by guests.

Kerrera Bunkhouse: Perched on a hill overlooking Loch Creran, Barcaldine Castle provides a singular and remarkable experience in a medieval environment. Visitors laud the castle's opulent lodgings, breathtaking vistas, and personal service.

Guests have praised these top-rated Oban lodgings for their outstanding service, cozy rooms, and handy locations.

Selecting Your Perfect Accommodation

Ensuring a pleasant and pleasurable stay in Oban requires careful selection of the ideal accommodation. With so many choices, it's critical to think about your tastes, spending limit, and kind of vacation. Remember the following while choosing the ideal lodging for you:

Location: Think about where the lodging is with respect to the sights and things you wish to do in Oban.

Whether a quiet country hideaway or a waterfront hotel with expansive views are more your style, pick a spot that works with your schedule and provides easy access to the attractions and services you want.

Amenities: List any freebies, recreational facilities, and on-site eating options that the lodging provides. Select lodging that satisfies your needs and decide which facilities—like a fitness center, free Wi-Fi, or a full Scottish breakfast—you really need for your stay.

Budget: Determine and then adhere to a budget for your lodging. From opulent resorts to reasonably priced guesthouses and hostels, Oban has lodging choices to fit every pocketbook. Decide what you can really afford, and search for lodging that provides the greatest value for your money.

Reviews And Ratings: To learn more about the general caliber and experience of the lodging, read reviews and ratings from past visitors. Seek for lodgings with great ratings for comfort, cleanliness, and customer service. Note any recurrent themes or problems that the reviews bring up that might have an impact on your visit.

Accessibility: When making your hotel reservation, be sure to ask about accessibility amenities including wheelchair ramps, elevators, and accessible rooms if you have particular accessibility needs or mobility issues. Select lodging that will meet your requirements and guarantee your comfort.

Packages And Special Offers: Watch for any packages, special offers, or discounts that could be accessible for the lodging you have selected. For reservations made in advance, stays of several nights, or during off-peak times, many hotels and guesthouses provide savings. Profit from these specials to get cheaper lodging.

Personal Preferences: While selecting lodging, keep in mind your own tastes and manner of travel. Select lodging that suits your tastes and improves your whole Oban experience, whether it's a modern hotel with slick design and facilities or a comfortable bed and breakfast with a homely feel.

Hints And Tips For Booking

With these pointers and techniques, reserving lodging in Oban may be simple and guarantee a seamless booking procedure:

Book Early: Particularly for busy events and high visitor seasons, book your Oban lodging well in advance to get the greatest prices and availability. Choosing the ideal place to stay is also made easier and more flexible when you book early.

Compare Prices: To compare the costs and features provided by various Oban lodgings, use comparison websites and online booking systems. Make the most of filters and sorting choices to focus your search and locate the top offers that fit your requirements.

Seek For Promotions: Look for any specials, discounts, or promotions that could be accessible for the lodging you have selected. For special offers and packages, visit the official website, social media accounts, and outside booking sites.

Consider Flexible Dates: Think About Adjusting Your Itinerary to Take Advantage of Cheaper Prices and Better Deals: If your trip dates are flexible, think about doing so. Be adaptable with your travel dates to save money on lodging; off-peak seasons and midweek stays are typically more economical.

Read The Fine Print: Before making a hotel reservation, go over the terms and conditions, cancellation policies, and any possible extra costs or taxes. Watch the booking specifics and make sure you know the policies and procedures in case of modifications or cancellations.

Make Direct Contact: If you have certain needs or preferences, think about making direct contact with the accommodation to go over your requirements and find out about any unique accommodations. This can help to guarantee that your needs are fulfilled and that any unique needs are taken care of while you are there.

Join Loyalty Programs: Sign up for membership clubs and loyalty programs provided by hotels and booking sites to receive points, prizes, and special privileges with every reservation. Utilize member-only specials, upgrades, and benefits to make the most of your visit and save money on next reservations.

Find the ideal lodging in Oban that suits your requirements, tastes, and budget by using these booking advice and techniques, and you'll have a wonderful and memorable stay in this quaint seaside town.

CHAPTER 4

OUTDOOR ADVENTURES

IN OBAN

An outdoor lover's dream come true, Oban lies tucked away on Scotland's west coast. There is no lack of adventure waiting for you in this charming seaside town, from exploring craggy coasts to heading into the Scottish Highlands.

We'll go into some of the most exciting outdoor pursuits Oban has to offer in this chapter, including hiking paths, sea kayaking, animal viewing, and cruises to the Isles.

Cruises To The Isles

Sail to the adjacent isles that encircle Oban to set off on an amazing adventure. These island tours provide a special chance to discover the rich history and breathtaking scenery of Scotland's western isles.

The following are some often visited island cruise destinations from Oban:

Isle Of Mull: Take a cruise to this island to see its varied scenery, which includes everything from craggy beaches and rocky coasts to peaceful lochs and high mountains. Take in the vibrant town of Tobermory, see old castles and ruins, and watch for seals, otters, and eagles.

Staffa And Fingal's Cave: Visit the deserted island of Staffa to take in the bizarre geological structures, which include the well-known Fingal's Cave. Travel the craggy coast, take a guided tour of the island, and hear the eerie echoes of the cave's inherent acoustics.

Iona: See the ancient abbey, burial places, and immaculate beaches of this holy island. Discover the island's religious significance and links to early Christianity, then meander slowly around the tranquil surroundings.

The Treshnish Isles: Explore the wild cliffs, sea caves, and profusion of birds of the isolated Treshnish Isles by boat. See razorbills, guillemots, and puffins nesting on the cliffs, and take in the breath-taking vistas of the surrounding waterscape.

Oban Bay Wildlife Cruises: See seals, dolphins, and porpoises playing in their natural habitat by taking a wildlife tour in Oban Bay and the nearby waterways. While taking in the picturesque vistas from the boat, learn about the local ecosystem and marine life from informed guides.

Discover the peace of Iona, the untamed vistas of Mull, or the geological marvels of Staffa—a cruise to the isles from Oban promises an amazing journey through some of Scotland's most spectacular terrain.

Hiking Trails

There are many different walking routes in Oban and the surrounding area that suit all fitness and experience levels. Every outdoor lover can enjoy a path, which ranges in difficulty from easy beach strolls to strenuous mountain excursions. Put on your hiking shoes and follow these best routes to discover Oban's natural beauty on foot:

Oban Bay Path: Saunter slowly along the path to take in the expansive vistas of the surrounding hills, islands, and port of the town. down the route, this simple coastal walk winds down the coast from Oban town center to Ganavan Sands, past scenic beaches, woods, and vistas.

Dunollie Woodland Walk: Take in the breathtaking views of Oban Bay from this picturesque walking route that winds through the old woodlands of Dunollie Estate. See historic sights like Dunollie Castle and the remains of St. Columba's Chapel as you meander through tranquil meadows, woodlands, and gardens.

Ben Lora Trail: Take on a strenuous climb of the well-known hill that commands a view of Oban. A relatively difficult climb through woodlands and moorland leads to the summit of the Ben Lora Trail, which rewards with expansive views of Oban, the nearby islands, and the mountains of Mull.

Ganavan Sands Coastal Walk: Savor breathtaking vistas of the Isle of Kerrera and the Firth of Lorn by following the coastal path from Ganavan Sands to Dunstaffnage Castle. With many excellent chances for birdwatching and wildlife sighting along the way, this easy-to-moderate walk winds past sandy beaches, rocky coasts, and grassy headlands.

Isle Of Kerrera Circular Walk: From Oban, take a quick ferry ride to the Isle of Kerrera, then set out on a picturesque circular walk around the island. Hike past historic sites like Gylen Castle and Hutcheson's Monument and along craggy cliffs for breath-taking vistas of Oban Bay, the Isle of Mull, and the surrounding coastline.

Oban has hiking routes to suit every aptitude and interest level, whether you're searching for a strenuous mountain trip or a relaxing beach stroll. Therefore, to fully appreciate the natural splendor of this breathtaking coastline area, put on your hiking boots, take a picnic, and hit the trails.

Sea Kayaking

Go sea kayaking to see Oban's immaculate coastline from an other angle. Discover the peace and beauty of Scotland's west coast as you paddle your way through protected bays, secret coves, and glistening clean waters.

Oban offers many of chances for experienced kayakers as well as novices to enjoy this thrilling water sport. You might like to try these sea kayaking adventures:

Half-Day Kayak Excursion: With knowledgeable instructors, take a guided half-day kayak excursion and explore the waters surrounding Oban. With informed guides teaching you about the history, animals, and ecology of the region, paddle along the coast, past famous sites, and through picturesque sea caves.

Full-Day Kayak Trip: Discover farther-off and more inaccessible parts of the shore by going on a full-day kayak trip. Travel to neighboring islands, undiscovered beaches, and remote bays and take advantage of the chances to observe wildlife and go snorkeling. Savor the breathtaking beauty all around you as you pause for a picnic lunch on a distant beach.

Sunset Kayak Tour: A guided kayak trip at sunset will let you to fully appreciate Oban's shoreline. As the sun sets and a golden glow covers the countryside, paddle out into the tranquil bay waters. Gliding on the lake, take in the sounds of nature and watch as the sky changes colors.

Multi-Day Kayaking Trip: Travel the west coast of Scotland on a multi-day kayaking trip for the best sea kayaking experience. See far-off islands, craggy shorelines, and secret sea lochs; camp on deserted beaches under the starlight. Escape into the wild and enjoy the independence of sea kayaking in one of Scotland's most stunning and isolated areas.

A special approach to appreciate the Scottish coast's unspoiled seas, profusion of animals, and breathtaking landscape is to go sea kayaking in Oban. Whatever your level of experience and preferences, there are rental and guided tour choices. So be ready to discover Oban's coastal treasures from the seat of a kayak by grabbing a paddle and donning a wetsuit.

Wildlife Watching

Oban and the surrounding waterways are a wildlife lover's dream come true. Discover a plethora of species in this coastal area, from elusive seabirds to magnificent marine creatures. To see some of Scotland's most famous and intriguing animals, take a guided wildlife-watching tour or set off on your own. Enjoy the following wildlife-watching activities in Oban:

Whale And Dolphin Watching: From Oban, take a boat trip out into the Inner Hebrides' broad waters in quest of whales and dolphins. Look for bottlenose, porpoises, and minke whales playing in the waves and talk to informed guides about their habits and conservation.

Seabird Spotting: Nesting on coastal cliffs and rocky outcrops are a number of seabird species, including razorbills, guillemots, and puffins, who call Oban home. See these seabird colonies up close and in their natural environment by boating to islands like Staffa and Lunga.

Seal Watching: A resident colony of harbor seals can be observed frequently soaking on rocky shores or bobbing in the water in Oban Bay and the adjacent waterways. Go on a guided boat trip or hire a kayak and paddle out to seal colonies to see these gregarious animals at play.

Birdwatching: See a great range of bird species by exploring the many habitats around Oban, which range from moorlands and coastal cliffs.

Look for waders, waterfowl, and songbirds in their native habitats as well as raptors like buzzards and golden eagles swooping overhead.

Red Deer Safaris: Experience one of Britain's most famous native animals on a guided red deer safari into the Scottish Highlands. Discover the ecology and behaviour of red deer as you explore their natural habitat and take advantage of chances for wildlife photography and observation.

The rich and varied ecology of Oban provides countless chances for environmental appreciation and wildlife observation. See and hear for the amazing variety of animals that makes this coastal region home whether you're hiking through the countryside, boating around the coast, or just taking in the views from a picturesque viewpoint.

A little luck and patience will guarantee that your trip in Oban will include some very remarkable animal experiences.

CHAPTER 5

DINING AND CULINARY EXPERIENCES

Called the "Seafood Capital of Scotland," Oban provides a delicious selection of restaurants and culinary experiences that highlight the area's rich culinary history.

Oban's eating scene will tempt your taste senses with anything from hearty Scottish cuisine and artisanal treats to fresh seafood collected daily in the nearby waters. T

he finest eating places and culinary experiences Oban has to offer—seafood eateries, traditional Scottish cuisine, cafés and bakeries, and whisky tasting experiences—will be covered in this chapter.

Seafood Restaurants

Being a seaside town on the Atlantic Ocean, Oban is well-known for its profusion of fresh seafood, which is the main attraction on the menus of its several eateries.

Succulent langoustines and plump scallops to delicate salmon and flaky haddock—Oban offers an abundance of mouthwatering seafood meals. Top seafood eateries to enjoy the tastes of the sea are as follows:

Ee-Usk: A seafood lover's dream come true, Ee-usk is situated on the beachfront with a view of Oban Bay. Offering a variety of delectable dishes, from traditional fish and chips to creative seafood platters and shellfish delicacies, this award-winning restaurant places a strong focus on responsibly obtained and locally sourced seafood. Savor delicious seafood treats and take in expansive views of the bay while dining al fresco on the restaurant's outside patio.

Cuan Mor: This modern seafood restaurant and bar in the centre of Oban honours the finest of Scottish food and friendliness. Offering a wide range of seafood classics and contemporary takes on the menu together with a choice of craft beers and whiskies, this busy restaurant has something for everyone. Savour the catch of the day, expertly cooked by the restaurant's skilled chefs, or sample the local oysters or a seafood chowder.

Coast: Tucked down in the charming village of Benderloch, a short drive from Oban, Coast is a little-known treasure renowned for its delicious seafood and breathtaking views of the surrounding coastline. Showcasing the finest of Scotland's larder, the restaurant's menu features everything from pan-seared sea bass and grilled lobster to hand-dived scallops and West Coast mussels. Savor the peaceful atmosphere and kind welcome whether you dine in the restaurant's fine dining room or on the outside patio.

Waterfront Fishouse Restaurant: Offering a singular dining experience with unmatched views of the sea, the restaurant is perched on the edge of Oban's North Pier, overlooking the busy harbour. Savor a range of just caught seafood, masterfully cooked by the restaurant's talented chefs, including West Coast oysters, langoustines, and Loch

Fyne salmon. Toast to the flavours of the sea with a glass of wine or a dram of whisky from the vast drinks menu.

Traditional Scottish Fare

Apart from its seafood selection, Oban boasts a range of eateries and restaurants that serve up traditional Scottish cuisine, highlighting the rich culinary customs of the Highlands and Islands.

Every taste can be satiated by anything from rich stews and savoury pies to delicate pastries and sweets. Here are some of Oban's best places to eat traditional Scottish food:

The Olive Garden: A cozy café renowned for its kind service and hearty Scottish cuisine, The Olive Garden is tucked away on a quaint cobblestone street in Oban's town centre. Savor substantial fare such deer stew, Scotch soup, and haggis neeps and tatties, all prepared using locally obtained ingredients and presented with a hearty helping of Scottish friendliness. Try a classic cranachan or sticky toffee pudding to finish your dinner.

The Seafood Temple: This little treasure, which specializes in modernized classic Scottish seafood dishes, is situated on the outskirts of Oban and overlooks the picturesque Sound of Kerrera. Sample specialties including Argyll lamb, Cullen skink, and smoked haddock and potato soup, all served with a choice of seasonal vegetables and locally obtained ingredients. Savor the tranquil atmosphere and breathtaking views while you eat and have a glass of wine or a pint of ale from the restaurant's large drink menu.

Piazza: A family-friendly restaurant and café dishing up traditional Scottish fare as well as worldwide favorites, Piazza is located in the centre of Oban. There's something on the menu for everyone, from substantial steak and ale pie to classic haggis, neeps and tatties. Indulging in a sweet treat with a cup of tea or coffee is made possible by the restaurant's assortment of freshly baked cakes and pastries.

The Oban Inn: Situated in the middle of Oban, this historic tavern and restaurant dates back to the eighteenth centuries. Enjoying a taste of Scotland's culinary legacy is made easy with its warm ambiance, classic décor, and friendly service. Savor traditional fare such stovies, bangers and mash, and fisherman's pie, all accompanied with a pint of locally produced ale or a whisky from the large drinks menu.

Cafés And Bakeries

Delicious pastries, handcrafted delicacies, and freshly brewed coffee are all available in the quaint cafés and bakeries in Oban. These quaint restaurants will fulfill your sweet tooth whether you're in the mood for a leisurely breakfast, a mid-afternoon pick-me-up, or a cake. Visit these excellent bakeries and cafés in Oban:

Oban Chocolate Company: Savour a rich chocolatey treat at this town centre location of Oban. Along with freshly produced coffee and hot chocolate prepared with real Scottish milk, this artisanal chocolate shop and café serves a delectable selection of handcrafted chocolates, truffles, and confections. Savor a chocolate cake slice or assortment of chocolates to go and eat.

The Little Potting Shed Café: Tucked away in the peaceful surrounds of Oban's Rockfield Centre, The Little Potting Shed Café offers a haven from the activity of the town centre. Tucked away in a quaint garden shed, this little café provides a laid-back vibe together with a variety of freshly baked pastries, cakes, and small snacks. Nestled within a beautiful garden, it's the ideal place to take a leisurely breakfast or lunch in the middle of the outdoors.

As you take in the tranquil atmosphere, have a warm scone with jam and cream or a slice of freshly baked cake with a cup of freshly brewed coffee or tea.

Oban Bay Coffee Company: Visit this well-liked café and roastery on Oban's North Pier to get your day started. Taste the rich aroma of just roasted coffee beans while you enjoy a cup of well brewed coffee prepared using beans that are obtained locally. From the café's waterfront setting, take in expansive views of the harbor and neighboring islands while sipping your coffee with a freshly crafted croissant or breakfast sandwich prepared with locally sourced ingredients.

Nories Café: Nestled in the center of Oban, this quaint retro-style café will transport you back in time. A taste of traditional Scottish hospitality may be had here with its charming service, nostalgic atmosphere, and classic décor. Savor a traditional afternoon tea, handmade soup, or a filling breakfast all presented on antique china and complemented by a variety of pastries and cakes.

Bakery Cafe: This little treasure, tucked away on a side street in Oban's town center, is well-known for its mouthwatering baked bread, pastries, and cakes.

Come have a slice of cake prepared using ingredients found locally, a variety of sweet and savory pastries, or a freshly baked loaf of bread. Enjoy your delicacies to go while touring Oban's streets, or sit at one of the café's comfortable tables.

Whisky Tasting

Without trying the most well-known export of Scotland, whiskey, no trip there would be complete. Tucked down in the heart of Scotland's whisky-producing region, Oban provides many of chances to sample and discover this legendary drink. Regardless of your level of expertise with whiskies, these tasting events will tantalize your senses:

Oban Distillery: Take a guided tour of this famous single malt whisky's production process. Explore the old distillery with its classic copper pot stills and learn about the distillation process from malting and mashing to fermentation and maturation. A guided tasting of Oban's finest whiskies, including the age-old Oban 14 Year Old, will help you to fully understand the complexity and personality of Scotch whisky.

Whiskey Bars: Oban has a number of whiskey bars where you may try a variety of Scotch whiskies from Scottish distilleries. Savor the wide selection of single malts, blends, and uncommon bottlings on the whiskey menus at The Lorne Bar and the Oban Inn. Drinking drams of your favorite whiskies and discovering new ones along the way, have conversations with the friendly bartenders and other whisky lovers.

Whisky Tasting Experiences: Without leaving Oban, take a trip around Scotland's whisky areas with a skilled whisky specialist leading a tasting experience. Discover the background, making process, and tasting notes of each whisky as you sample a range of whiskies from many distilleries that each highlight the distinctive flavors and qualities of its own area. Whether your tastes run to fruity Speyside whiskies, peaty Islay malts, or strong Highland drams, there is a tasting experience to suit them.

Whisky Festivals and Events: Keep a look out for all of the year-round whisky festivals and events in and around Oban. Whisky tastings and seminars, distillery visits and special releases—these events provide a singular chance to become fully immersed in the world of Scotch whisky and meet other whisky lovers.

Meet the creators of the companies, sample uncommon and limited-edition whiskies, and learn about the skill and art of Scottish whisky making.

You'll learn to appreciate Scotland's national drink and its rich history and customs more no matter which whiskey tasting session you choose.

CHAPTER 6

SHOPPING IN OBAN

With so many outlets to suit every taste and inclination, Oban provides a wonderful shopping experience.

This little seaside town has everything you could possibly need, whether you're looking for specialist items, fresh fruit, locally produced crafts, or unusual souvenirs.

We'll look at the top shopping destinations in Oban in this chapter, ranging from specialist stores and craft boutiques to local markets and souvenir shops.

Souvenir Shops

Souvenir stores are the ideal spot to buy mementos and keepsakes to remember your stay if you want to bring a little bit of Oban's charm home.

From unusual presents and funny goods to classic Scottish plaid, these stores have a large selection of mementos to suit every taste. Explore the following excellent gift stores in Oban:

Oban Whisky and Fine Wines Shop: The Oban Whisky and Fine Wines Shop is a great place to bring a little bit of Scotland home with you. It is situated in the centre of Oban. Look through their selection of excellent Scottish whiskies—which includes blends, single malts, and limited-edition releases—and grab a bottle to share with loved ones or as a unique present for a whisky enthusiast.

Oban Chocolate Company: Savour a delectable keepsake from this delightful selection of handcrafted chocolates, truffles, and candies. Savor a box of handcrafted chocolates prepared with products found locally, or choose a variety of sweets to give to family and friends back home.

The Tartan Shop: Enter and find a veritable gold mine of Scottish tartan, kilts and accessories. View their collection of clan crests and traditional tartan patterns to choose the ideal memento to remember your trip to Scotland. This store offers items for everyone, whether of Scottish heritage or just love tartan.

Oban Distillery Gift Store: Don't miss the opportunity to purchase a bottle of Oban whisky or other whisky-themed mementos at the gift store following your tour of the distillery. Whisky-flavored candies and fudge to branded glasses and bar accessories—there are lots of unusual presents to take home and remember your distillery experience.

Local Markets

See one of Oban's humming markets for a sample of the local cuisine and an opportunity to interact with the locals. These markets provide a lively shopping experience unmatched by others, with everything from fresh vegetables and specialty cuisine to handcrafted goods and unusual presents. Following are some Oban markets you really should not miss:

Oban Farmer's Market: Showcasing the finest of Argyll's regional produce, artisanal foods, and handmade crafts, the market is held on a few days of the year. Savor a range of products as you meander around the market stalls, including baked goods, artisan cheeses, fresh fruits and vegetables, and homemade jams and preserves. Speak with the amiable sellers to find out about the origins of their goods and to purchase some delectable delicacies to enjoy while in Oban or to give as presents.

Oban Indoor Market: Tucked up in the center of Oban, this lively marketplace is home to merchants offering everything from jewelry and clothes to artwork and antiques. Look through the booths to find a wide variety of items, such as unique mementos, vintage finds, and handcrafted items. This vibrant market has everything you could possibly need, whether it be a special gift for a loved one, a quirky trinket, or a distinctive piece of jewelry.

Oban Artisan Market: Handmade crafts and artisanal products aficionados should not miss this monthly event, which takes place in the picturesque surrounds of Station Square. Explore the booths and take in the creations of regional artists, who display their skills in woodworking, textiles, pottery, and other media. There is something at this lively market for everyone, from handmade jewelry and accessories to unusual home décor items.

Craft Boutiques

Oban's craft boutiques are the ideal place for anyone looking for locally made products and handcrafted treasures. These little stores offer a well-chosen assortment of wearable art, home décor, and handcrafted gifts while showcasing the skills of regional craftspeople. Explore these craft stores in Oban:

Sea Tangle Studio: Nestled in the centre of Oban, this sanctuary for fans of handcrafted goods and coastal-inspired décor is a must-visit. View their selection of handcrafted textiles, artwork, and ceramics, all influenced by the stunning Scottish coastline. Everything from screen-printed textiles and hand-painted pottery to driftwood sculptures and sea glass jewelry is a distinct representation of Oban's maritime past.

Sorcha Crafts: This family-owned store specializes in Scottish mementos and handmade gifts and is housed in a historic building with a view of Oban Bay. Enter and browse through their assortment of regionally produced crafts, which includes artwork, pottery, knitwear, and more. At Sorcha Crafts, you can find anything from a decorative ceramic piece to a warm wool sweater to a one-of-a-kind artwork to hang on your walls.

Tweed And Tartan: This shop devoted to Scotland's famous textiles will let you to experience the classic elegance of tweed and tartan. Explore their selection of tweed jackets, kilts, scarves and accessories, all expertly woven from the best Scottish wool. This chic store has both contemporary tartan scarves and classic Harris Tweed jackets.

Specialty Stores

Numerous specialized shops in Oban provide one-of-a-kind items and gourmet delicacies unavailable elsewhere. Specialty shops serve discriminating customers seeking for something unique with everything from luxury items and handcrafted crafts to artisanal meals and excellent wines. Visit these specialist shops in Oban:

The Green Room: Savour your senses in the town center specialty food store and deli, The Green Room.

Gather up gourmet treats like handcrafted chocolates, artisan cheeses, locally cured salmon, and gourmet condiments—all ideal for preparing a gourmet dinner at home or picnic. Before you go, be sure to try some of the store's delectable chocolates and get a bottle of wine or whisky to go with your dinner.

Oban Fine Wines: An international treasure trove of fine wines, spirits, and liqueurs awaits wine connoisseurs and aficionados. Peruse their well-chosen assortment of whiskies, champagnes, and wines and enable their friendly staff to assist you in selecting the ideal bottle for any occasion. Oban Fine Wines has everything you need to commemorate a milestone with a special vintage or locate a one-of-a-kind present for a wine lover.

The Tartan Company: Enter The Tartan Company to experience Scottish elegance and history. Offering a carefully chosen assortment of premium items crafted from the best wool and textiles, this business specializes in tartan apparel, accessories, and presents. View their selection of tartan shawls, ties, kilts, and scarves, all made by expert craftspeople using age-old methods. The Tartan Company has a garment you'll treasure whether you want to acknowledge your Scottish heritage or just enjoy tartan's classic elegance.

The Chocolate Box: This specialized boutique offers handcrafted chocolates and confections prepared with the best ingredients. Indulge yourself in a little luxury. Savor a range of expertly made pralines, truffles and artisanal chocolates. There is something at The Chocolate Box to sate every appetite, from traditional milk chocolate bars to unusual fruit-filled truffles.

Oban Art Gallery: Visit this boutique exhibiting the creations of regional artists and craftspeople to fully experience Oban's thriving arts community. View the wide variety of styles and techniques on exhibit as you peruse their collection of paintings, sculptures, ceramics, and fabrics. Oban Art Gallery will excite you whether you are an experienced art collector or just value exquisite workmanship.

With everything from gourmet meals and luxury items to mementos and regional crafts, Oban's specialty shops provide a distinctive shopping experience that highlights the finest of Scottish artistry and skill. Take your time, peruse the stores, and find things to bring back from your stay to this little seaside town.

We'll go into Oban's rich history and cultural legacy in the next chapter, looking at its intriguing past and the sites that help to define it. Come learn the tales behind Oban's historic sights, which include both contemporary structures that influence the town's beauty and character as well as old castles and monuments.

CHAPTER 7

DAY TRIPS FROM OBAN

Exploring the surrounding breathtaking scenery, historic sites, and quaint villages is made easy from Oban. Adventures abound within a short distance from the town, from craggy beaches and towering mountains to historic castles and charming lochs.

We'll look carefully at some of the top day trips from Oban in this chapter, each of which offers a special fusion of outdoor activities, cultural history, and scenic beauty.

Isle Of Mull

Oban is only a short boat trip away from the Isle of Mull, an outdoor and nature lover's dream come true. Mull presents countless chances for adventure and discovery with its craggy shoreline, undulating hills, and varied fauna.

Highlights of a day trip to the Isle of Mull include:

Tobermory: Discover the vibrantly painted buildings, quaint port, and busy shoreline of this vibrant town to begin your day excursion. Wander the waterfront walkway, peruse the galleries and stores, and stop by the Tobermory Distillery to try some of the best whisky on the island.

Mull Eagle Watch: Join Mull Eagle Watch for a guided eagle-watching excursion to see one of Mull's most famous residents. Go into the island's lonely and untamed landscapes with professional guides in pursuit of golden and white-tailed eagles as well as other natural animals including red deer, otters, and seals.

Fingal's Cave: Just off the coast of Mull, on the deserted island of Staffa, take in the natural wonder of this sea cave. The stunning cave, which is flanked by towering cliffs and formed of hexagonal basalt columns, is accessible by boat from Mull's coastlines.

Duart Castle: This magnificent stronghold built on a cliff overlooking the Sound of Mull is a trip through time. Discover the history of the castle, take in the breathtaking vistas from the battlements, and discover the centuries-long Maclean family who have lived at Duart Castle.

Isle Of Staffa

A short boat trip from the Isle of Mull, Staffa is a little, deserted island well-known for its spectacular basalt columns and underwater caverns. A trip to Staffa provides an opportunity to take in some of Scotland's most spectacular natural landscape.

See and do the following on a day excursion to the Isle of Staffa:

Fingal's Cave: Recognized for its hexagonal basalt columns and unsettling acoustics, this magnificent sea cave is the high point of any trip to Staffa. Board a boat to the island and get off at the landing stage to go on foot exploration of the cave and take in its breathtaking splendor.

Wildlife Watching: With so much marine life in the waters surrounding Staffa, keep a watch out for wildlife while you sail there. Seabirds breeding on the cliffs include puffins, guillemots, and razorbills; seals are also seen lounging on the rocks and dolphins are seen playing in the surf.

Am Buachaille: If feeling daring, think about scaling Staffa's highest point, Am Buachaille. Awe at the island's untamed beauty and expansive views of the surrounding sea and shore will greet you at the summit.

Glencoe

Step inland from Oban to see Glencoe, one of the most famous and spectacular scenery in Scotland.

Tucked up in the Scottish Highlands, Glencoe is well-known for its imposing mountains, enveloping glens, and stormy past.

Discover the following on a day trip to Glencoe:

Hiking: To go on foot exploration of Glencoe, lace up your boots and hit the paths. Select from a range of hiking paths that suit all ability levels, from easy strolls along glen floors to strenuous climbs up steep ridges. Hiking favorites include the Buachaille Etive Mor, the Devil's Staircase, and Lost Valley.

Visitor Center: Nestled in the middle of the glen, the Glencoe Visitor Center offers information about the history, geology, and animals of Glencoe.

View educational films, peruse interactive displays, and speak with informed staff members who may offer guidance and pointers for seeing the region.

Photography: Photographers will find heaven in Glencoe with its breathtaking scenery and constantly shifting light. Take a camera and photograph the glen during sunrise or sunset, when the surrounding scenery is most evocative and the mountains are illuminated by golden light.

Inveraray

Beautifully located on the banks of Loch Fyne, Inveraray is renowned for its rich cultural legacy, stunning scenery, and medieval buildings.

Discover historic sites, take part in outdoor pursuits, and fully experience Scottish culture with a day trip to Inveraray.

See and do the following in Inveraray:

Inveraray Castle: Visit the magnificent gardens and interiors of Inveraray Castle, the Duke of Argyll's family residence. Wandering around the lavish halls and exquisitely designed grounds, take in the castle's magnificent architecture, elaborate furnishings, and remarkable art collection.

Inveraray Jail: Take a trip through time at this living museum, which provides an intriguing look into Scotland's criminal past. View the old courthouse, jail cells, and displays that tell about the life of staff members and inmates in the 1800s.

Loch Fyne: Saunter slowly around the loch's banks to take in its serene beauty. See the surrounding mountains and forests, and keep a look out for wildlife like otters, seals, and seabirds.

Shopping And Dining: Peruse the galleries and stores in the quaint town center of Inveraray, which offers a range of regional goods, presents, and mementos. After that, unwind in one of the town's traditional pubs or quaint tearooms and have some excellent Scottish food and seafood that is caught nearby.

Day excursions from Oban include a wide variety of experiences that highlight Scotland's natural beauty, cultural legacy, and outdoor activities, from island adventures to mountain treks and historic sites.

Every place you visit—the untamed shoreline of Mull, the geological marvels of Staffa, the hiking in the magnificent mountains of Glencoe, or the history and charm of Inveraray—promises an unforgettable day of discovery.

CHAPTER 8

FESTIVALS AND EVENTS IN OBAN

The rich history and breathtaking scenery of Oban are well-known, but so are its thriving cultural scene and year-round festivals and events.

This seaside town never sleeps, with everything from music festivals and agricultural displays to traditional Highland games. We'll go into some of Oban's most well-known festivals and events in this chapter, each of which provides a special window into the local way of life and culture.

Oban Winter Festival

The Oban Winter Festival, which celebrates everything winter and offers a ton of events and activities for people of all ages, is a great way to start the festive season.

There is a plenty to see and do at this wonderful time of year, from live music and seasonal entertainment to traditional markets and craft fairs. At the Oban Winter Festival, anticipate the following:

Christmas Market: Peruse the booths at the Oban Christmas Market to find unusual presents, handcrafted goods, and joyous delicacies from regional makers and sellers. There are many more items to check off your holiday buying list, from hand-knitted sweaters and woolen scarves to handcrafted preserves and artisanal chocolates.

Street Food Festival: Savor delectable global fare created by regional chefs and food merchants at the Oban Street Food Festival. Gourmet burgers and wood-fired pizzas to real Thai food and freshly shucked oysters—this culinary feast has something to satisfy every appetite.

Live Music Events: Take in live music events at pubs, bars, and outdoor stages across Oban by regional bands and musicians. The festival program includes pop and rock from today's top artists as well as traditional Scottish folk music.

Community Events: Participate in the holiday cheer with a range of neighborhood gatherings and events, such as tree lighting ceremonies, carol singing, and Santa's grotto visits. Explore the quaint streets of Oban decked with lights and decorations and bring the whole family to fully experience the holiday mood.

Highland Games

A cherished centuries-old Scottish custom, the Highland Games honor the nation's exceptional athletic and cultural legacy. Annually held in towns and villages all over Scotland, including Oban, the Highland Games are a display of power, talent, and friendship as competitors compete in classic Scottish sports like tug-of-war, hammer throwing, and caber tossing. At the Oban Highland Games, anticipate the following:

Athletic Events: Take in the caber toss, stone throw, weight throw, and hammer throw among other traditional Highland sports as competitors from all around Scotland and beyond compete. Watch as the competitors in these age-old competitions of endurance and strength battle for glory.

Pipe Band Performances: Take in the energizing bagpipes as pipe bands from all across the area compete in energetic musical performances. The bands marching and playing add to the joyous mood of the games; listen to the eerie tunes and booming drumbeats.

Traditional Dancing: Enjoy the vibrant reels and complex choreography of Scottish traditional dancers to the accompaniment of accordions and fiddles. Try your hand (or feet) at some Highland dancing to join in the festivities, or just watch from the sidelines.

Food And Craft Stalls: Stroll around the games field's food and craft stalls to find a range of artisanal and handcrafted items as well as delectable delicacies. The Highland Games provide something for everyone, from freshly prepared pies and filling stews to tartan kilts and handcrafted jewelry.

Oban Live Music Festival

Apologists for music rejoice! Highlight of the town's cultural calendar, the Oban Live Music Festival presents the finest Scottish and international musical talent in a series of thrilling shows and concerts.

Jazz and blues to folk and rock, there is a musical taste for everyone at the event. This is what to anticipate from Oban Live:

Headline Acts: As some of the biggest stars in the music business hit the stage to wow the audience with their spectacular performances, be ready to rock out. All ages of music lovers will be delighted by the roster, which includes chart-topping bands and renowned solo artists.

Local Talent: See the abundance of musical ability Scotland has to offer as regional bands and musicians perform live. The event gives up-and-coming indie bands as well as seasoned folk musicians a stage on which to present their music to a larger audience.

Outside Events: Take in the festival vibe with events and concerts outside in picturesque settings all around Oban.

With live music and the town's lovely shoreline and breathtaking natural surrounds as your backdrop, dance the night away under the stars.

Late-Night Sessions: Jam sessions and late-night sessions held in bars and pubs around Oban will keep the party going. Come along and enjoy the dynamic environment that is created by musicians coming together to perform impromptu sets and unexpected collaborations.

Highland Cattle Show

Don't miss the Oban Highland Cattle Show if you want a feel of rural Scotland and an opportunity to view some of the most famous animals up close.

Known for its unique shaggy coats, magnificent horns, and kind disposition, the Highland breed of cattle is honored at this yearly agricultural festival.

See and do the following during the Highland Cattle Show:

Cattle Judging: See breeders present their prized Highland cattle in a number of contests and judging sessions.

As these gorgeous animals parade around the show ring, competing for top awards in categories like best bull, best cow, and best young handler, take in their beauty and majesty.

Livestock Exhibitions: The event includes exhibitions of sheep, goats, and pigs in addition to Highland cattle. Wander amid the pens and paddocks, taking in the various breeds and discovering their distinctive traits, and marvel at the diversity of Scotland's agricultural history.

Crafts And Produce: At the Highland Cattle Show, peruse the food vendors' and craft stalls for a range of locally prepared meals and beverages as well as handcrafted items. Everyone will find something at the event, from hand-knitted sweaters and fuzzy socks to home-made jams and preserves.

Educational Demonstrations: Throughout the day, a number of educational demonstrations and workshops will teach you about traditional farming methods and rural living in Scotland. See expert craftspeople display methods including blacksmithing, wool spinning, and sheep shearing to get an understanding of the abilities and customs that have molded Scotland's agricultural past.

Everyone may enjoy one of Oban's festivals and events, which range from joyous festivities and cultural events to agricultural displays and music festivals.

CHAPTER 9

FAMILY-FRIENDLY

ACTIVITIES

Families may enjoy a variety of activities together in Oban, which is not simply a destination for adults.

There's enough to amuse every member of the family, from discovering aquatic life to enjoying sweets and outdoor pursuits.

The greatest family-friendly activities in Oban that will make enduring memories for everyone will be covered in this chapter.

Sealife Sanctuary

Head to the Scottish SEA LIFE Sanctuary in Oban for an engaging and educational family day out. The intriguing sea life at this marine conservation facility includes everything from gregarious otters and playful seals to vibrant fish and captivating jellyfish.

Here's what to anticipate from the Sealife Sanctuary:

Interactive Exhibits: Discover the varied marine species that calls Scotland's coastal seas home by exploring the aquarium's interactive exhibits. All ages will find lots to see and do, from underwater tunnels where you can watch sharks and rays glide above to touch pools where you can get up close to starfish and crabs.

Seal Feeding Sessions: Don't miss the daily feeding sessions when you may observe as knowledgeable personnel feeds the sanctuary's resident seals. Find more about these amazing animals and their innate habits, then be amazed by their dexterity and intellect as they play and do tricks in the water.

Attend educational conservation seminars and presentations given by specialists in animal care and marine biology. Find out how you may support the sanctuary's conservation efforts to save marine environments and animals.

Outdoor Play Area: Let the youngsters burn off some energy in the outdoor play area, which has slides, climbing frames, and other entertaining features, after touring the indoor displays. The kids run, jump, and play till they are full, so unwind and have a picnic in the sun.

Paddleboarding Lessons

Take the family paddleboarding on Oban Bay's immaculate waves and feel the rush. Families wishing to try something new together will find paddleboarding to be the ideal enjoyable and approachable water sport that is appropriate for all age groups and skill levels.

Expect the following from Oban paddleboarding lessons:

Safety Briefing and Instruction: Start your paddleboarding journey with a session of instruction and safety briefing given by certified instructors. Discover how to balance, paddle, and steer your board as well as the fundamentals of paddleboarding technique and important water safety advice.

Guided Tours: Take a guided paddleboarding trip to see Oban Bay's picturesque coastline from a different angle. Seek out animals including seals, seabirds, and perhaps even dolphins or porpoises as you paddle past craggy cliffs, remote coves, and stunning islands.

Family-Friendly Equipment: Select from a variety of tandem boards and inflatable SUPs made for kids that are family-friendly paddleboards made to fit many riders. The smallest family members can participate in the fun and love paddling on the water with the assistance of knowledgeable instructors.

Fun And Games: With games and activities for the whole family to enjoy, make the most of your time on the water. Play tag, race against one other, or just paddle about and explore at your own speed while taking in the sun and spending quality time in the great outdoors.

Oban Chocolate Company

Visit the Oban Chocolate Company to satisfy your sweet craving and spoil the whole family with a delectable selection of handcrafted chocolates and treats. This cherished local chocolatier has something to fulfill every appetite, from rich fudge and creamy truffles to rich chocolate bars and whimsical sweets.

This is what to anticipate from Oban Chocolate Company:

Chocolate Workshops: Discover the skill of making mouthwatering chocolates from scratch and let your imagination run wild. Mold, dip, and decorate your own chocolates under the direction of professional chocolatiers. Experiment with various flavors, fillings, and toppings to produce one-of-a-kind and customized delicacies.

Tasting Sessions: Savor some of the company's best chocolates and candies at a chocolate tasting session. Take in a sensory experience unlike any other as you learn about the subtleties of various cocoa beans, flavor profiles, and production methods.

Gift Shop: Stow sweets for your trip home in the little gift shop of the company. Select from a tempting selection of chocolate treats, expertly wrapped and prepared to give as a delectable memento of your visit to Oban, or to enjoy yourself.

Café: Indulge in a variety of delectable delicacies, including freshly made pastries, rich hot chocolates, and creamy milkshakes, in the company's little café. Savour your sweet treat while taking in the pleasant and warm ambiance of our family-friendly restaurant.

Oban Bay Play

Oban Bay Play is a family-friendly indoor soft play facility right in the town of Oban where the kids can let off some energy and have fun. Rain or shine, Oban Bay Play provides hours of enjoyment for kids of all ages with its vibrant play structures, ball pits and slides.

Oban Bay Play offers the following:

Soft Play Area: With a range of climbing frames, tunnels, and obstacles for children to explore, this area is perfect for a day of adventure and fun. See how they work their way through the vibrant play structures, hoovering, climbing, and sliding as they go, honing their coordination and motor abilities.

Toddler Zone: Created with smaller children in mind, the toddler zone provides a secure and engaging play and interaction space for young children. Under the careful observation of caring personnel, let them loose in the ball pit, crawl through the soft tunnels, or ride the small slides.

Café: Refuel and take a break from playtime at the café, which serves a variety of small meals, drinks and snacks. Knowing the children are having a fantastic time in a secure and watched setting, sit back and unwind while they play.

Birthday Parties: Oban Bay Play offers exclusive use of the play facilities and a special party area for you to celebrate your child's special day. Customized party packages including food, drinks, and entertainment are the ideal approach to make your child's birthday one they won't soon forget.

All ages will love the variety of family-friendly activities Oban has to offer, from discovering marine life and paddleboarding on the bay to indulging in sweets and burning off energy at the soft play area. This little seaside town offers lots of entertainment for families spending time together or for day trips with the kids.

CHAPTER 10

NIGHTLIFE IN OBAN

Oban's craggy coastline comes alive at night with a thriving entertainment scene that appeals to both residents and tourists.

Oban provides a wide range of evening entertainment choices, from exciting music venues presenting gifted artists to historic pubs offering excellent Scottish ales.

There's plenty to do after dark for everyone, whether your goals are to dance the night away to live music or relax with a beer by the fire.

We'll look at Oban's top pubs, bars, live music venues, whisky bars, and nightclubs in this chapter.

Pubs And Bars

There are many of friendly pubs and bars in Oban where you may have a good time with good company and a large drink menu. Every taste is catered for in a pub or bar, which ranges from modern establishments with waterfront views to traditional taverns with roaring fires.

Check out these top bars and pubs in Oban:

The Oban Inn: A typical Scottish pub with a kind welcome, The Oban Inn is tucked away in the middle of the town centre. Settle in at the bar, have a pint of locally produced ale or try one of the excellent whiskies while striking up a conversation with kind locals and other visitors.

The Waterfront Bar: With its commanding views of the port and beyond, The Waterfront Bar is perched above Oban Bay. Sit back with a glass of wine or a cocktail on the outside patio and take in the atmosphere while you watch the boats arrive and go. Regular live music events here enhance the vibrant atmosphere.

The Lorne Bar: Both residents and tourists love this quaint establishment with its Victorian-era furnishings. Enter, then take in the elaborate woodwork and stained glass windows while sipping from the well-stocked bar. Try the Lorne Lemonade, the pub's specialty cocktail, which is served with a twist and created using regional ingredients.

The Malt Whisky Bar: Featuring one of Oban's biggest collections of Scotch whisky, this is one place whisky enthusiasts won't want to miss. Savor and sip the tastes of Scotland's national drink from a vast selection of single malts, blends, and uncommon bottlings. Expert personnel is available to provide advice and suggestions to whisky consumers of all levels.

Live Music Venues

Oban is full with places where you may see gifted artists play anything from modern rock and pop to traditional Scottish folk. Every musical taste can be satisfied by anything from lively live bands to small quiet acoustic performances.

Following are some of Oban's best live music venues:

The View: Popular live music venue with a vibrant atmosphere and breathtaking views, The View is situated on the Esplanade facing Oban Bay. Local musicians will perform acoustic while you sip a drink and unwind, or when the band gets going, hit the dance floor.

The Corran Halls: From classical concerts and jazz performances to rock shows and tribute groups, this historic facility presents a wide range of live music events all year round. See what's happening when you visit the schedule to enjoy live music right in the center of Oban.

The Tyree Bar: Known for its open mic nights and live music events, The Tyree Bar is a hidden gem tucked away down side streets. As regional musicians hit the stage to perform, join in the excitement or take a seat at the bar and watch the entertainment while sipping a beer.

The Argyllshire Gathering Halls: You may enjoy the vibrant rhythms and traditional dances of Scotland on regular ceilidh nights held at this ancient site. Engage in the celebration as a caller leads you through the steps and a live band plays traditional music, guaranteeing to get your feet tapping.

Whisky Bars

Without trying some of Scotland's well-known whiskey, no trip to the nation would be complete, and Oban has a number of pubs where you can do just that. These whisky bars have a great range of drams to satisfy every taste, regardless of your level of experience with whisky or want to broaden your palate.

Following are some of Oban's best whiskey bars:

Ee-Usk: From well-known brands to uncommon and limited-edition bottlings, this waterfront restaurant and bar offers a vast selection of Scottish whiskies. Settle down at the bar and enable the informed personnel to lead you through the options as you come across both new and oldies.

Cuan Mor: A chic bar and restaurant with a well-stocked whisky cabinet, Cuan Mor is housed in a renovated church with a view of Oban Bay. Select from more than 100 whiskies from Scottish distilleries, including Oban's own, then have a dram in this elegantly restored building.

The Oban Whisky and Fine Wines Shop: Visit The Oban Whisky and Fine Wines Shop to peruse a large selection of whiskies and other spirits to take home with you if you would rather enjoy your whisky in the privacy of your own accommodation. Here you can find a wide selection of choices whether you are looking for a unique present for a whisky-loving buddy or a memento bottle to remember your trip.

Nightclubs

Oban has a couple of nightclubs where you may let free and party till the early hours of the morning for those who want to dance the night away. Even if the town may not have as many clubs as other cities, individuals looking for some nighttime entertainment will find these places to be active and entertaining.

Top nightclubs in Oban include the following:

The Corryvreckan: The Corryvreckan nightclub, so named after the well-known whirlpool off the coast of Jura, is a popular place for both residents and tourists to mingle and dance. It's the ideal spot to let your hair down and dance till morning with a DJ playing the newest music and a vibrant partygoer base.

The Skipinnish Ceilidh House: For a more traditional Scottish night out, spend it dancing the ceilidh and listening to live music at The Skipinnish Ceilidh House. As a caller walks you through the routines and a live band plays traditional music, everyone will be sure to get up and dance. Join in the excitement.

CHAPTER 11

WELLNESS AND

RELAXATION

Finding quiet and renewal times is crucial in the busy town of Oban, where the roaring waves meet the craggy coastline.

Chapter 11 looks at all the different ways to indulge in health and relaxation, from opulent spa trips to energizing outdoor pursuits.

Spa Retreats

At one of Oban's opulent spa resorts, escape the daily grind and lose yourself in a world of pampered pleasure.

Relaxing facials and revitalizing massages are just two of the therapies available at these havens that are meant to relieve tension and leave you feeling renewed.

The Spa at Isle Of Eriska Hotel: Situated on a secluded island a short drive from Oban, the Isle of Eriska Hotel features an excellent spa with a variety of luxurious treatments set against stunning natural surroundings. Take a hot stone massage, unwind in the sauna and steam room, or swim in the heated indoor pool with a view of the peaceful waters of Loch Linnhe.

The Lochside Hotel Spa: Tucked down on the banks of Loch Fyne, this is the ideal spot to relax and refuel. Savour a body wrap, a holistic massage, or just unwind in the outdoor hot tub while taking in the tranquilly of the Scottish countryside.

The Spa at The Perle Oban Hotel: Tucked away in the centre of Oban, The Perle Oban Hotel provides a tranquil spa experience with an array of opulent treatments to select from. From revitalizing facials to aromatherapy massages, every treatment is designed to calm the body, mind, and spirit so you emerge feeling utterly at ease and restored.

Yoga Studios

At one of Oban's friendly yoga studios, discover your inner zen and develop a feeling of peace and balance.

These studios provide a variety of classes appropriate for all skill levels of yogis, enabling you to re-establish your connection with yourself and find tranquilly in the middle of daily stress.

Oban Yoga: Offering a range of sessions to suit every requirement, from dynamic vinyasa flow to soothing hatha yoga, Oban Yoga is situated in the centre of Oban. Experienced teachers will lead you through each practice so you come away feeling centered, balanced, and prepared to face whatever comes your way.

The Studio: Offering a variety of yoga courses meant to support physical, mental, and emotional well-being, The Studio is tucked away in a serene setting with a view of Oban Bay. There is a class at this friendly studio to meet your requirements whether you want to become more flexible, less stressed, or just enjoy some quiet time.

Yoga By the Sea: As you practice yoga by the sea, take in the calming sound of the waves and the soft air. Yoga by the Sea, which is situated on the banks of Loch Linnhe, provides outdoor yoga courses in an amazing natural environment that let you flow through your practice while gaining inner calm.

Outdoor Wellness Activities

Accept the therapeutic potential of the natural world and lose yourself in outdoor wellness pursuits among Oban's stunning surroundings.

There are plenty of ways to feed your body, mind, and soul in this stunning region of Scotland, whether your tastes run to trekking through old woodlands, meditation by peaceful lochs, or yoga on remote beaches.

Forest Bathing: Take a forest bath in the ancient woodlands that round Oban to really experience the healing power of nature. A licensed forest therapy guide will lead you on a soothing sensory tour into the forest where you will practice mindfulness and make a profoundly meaningful connection with the natural world.

Meditation By the Loch: Take a seat beside one of Oban's stunning lochs and become lost in the tranquilly of the Scottish countryside. Deep relaxation and reflection are best facilitated by the tranquil surrounds, whether you decide to follow a guided meditation or sit in silent contemplation.

Beach Yoga: As you practice yoga on one of Oban's stunning beaches, feel the soft sea wind on your skin and the sand between your toes. Beach yoga provides a special chance to commune with the natural world and discover inner tranquilly with the sound of the waves serving as your soundtrack and the salty air energizing your senses.

Wellness Seminars

Take a wellness retreat or workshop in Oban to broaden your knowledge and grasp of comprehensive wellbeing. From self-care and nutrition to mindfulness and meditation, these seminars provide insightful information and useful skills for improving your general health and leading a more contented and balanced life.

Mindfulness Retreat: Discover how to develop present, awareness, and compassion in your everyday life by attending a mindfulness retreat guided by seasoned teachers and practitioners. By means of guided meditation, mindful movement, and group talks, you will delve into the principles of mindfulness and acquire useful abilities for stress management and achieving increased tranquilly and contentment.

Nutrition Course: Through mindful eating and nourishing cuisine, learn about the potential of food as medicine in this course that promotes maximum health and energy. Discover how to make tasty and nourishing dishes using locally grown, seasonal crops and get simple advice on how to include more plant-based foods in your diet for better energy, digestion, and general health.

Self-Care Retreat: Give yourself the gift of a retreat tailored to help you reestablish your connection with yourself and give your health first priority. With everything from light yoga and meditation to decadent spa treatments and artistic expression, these retreats provide a comprehensive approach to self-care that feeds the body, mind, and spirit, leaving you feeling reenergized and ready to face life again.

It's more critical than ever to put our health and wellness first in a world that frequently seems hectic and fast-paced. Oban provides a range of wellness experiences to support you in nourishing your body, mind, and soul, whether your goals are relaxation, renewal, or just a moment of calm among the chaos.

CHAPTER 12

LOCAL ETIQUETTE AND CUSTOMS

To make your visit to the little town of Oban go as smoothly and joyfully as possible, you should become acquainted with the local manners and traditions.

Respecting the customs and values of the people will help you not only negotiate contacts with them but also traverse them.

We'll go into detail on everything from greetings and civility to eating manners and tipping customs in this chapter.

Greetings And Courtesy

As in much of Scotland, Oban values friendliness and civility highly, and greetings are a crucial part of social interactions. An easy "hello" or "good morning" will typically do when you first meet someone or walk into a store or restaurant.

In more relaxed circumstances, a nod or smile is equally appropriate as a handshake.

In addressing someone, it's usual to use their title and last name, then "Mr." or "Ms." For instance, "Mr. Smith" or "Ms. MacLeod." If you're not sure what someone's title is, it's advisable to err on the side of formality until you're invited to use their first name.

Making eye contact and striking up small chat—like asking about someone's day or remarking on the weather—is considered courteous in social settings. Because Scots are renowned for their friendliness and hospitality, don't be shocked if complete strangers start talking to you in public.

Leaving, it's usual to say "goodbye" or "cheerio" and express gratitude for their time or help. Respect and thanks may also be expressed with a kind smile and a nod of the head.

Tipping Customs

Like the rest of the UK, Oban has comparable tipping customs; although not usually expected, gratuities are valued for really good service.

If you've had good service, it's usual to tip between 10% and 15% of the entire bill in bars and restaurants. Tipping more is not required, though, if the bill includes a service charge.

It is courteous to round up the price or leave a little tip for additional services, such hotel porters or taxi rides. It's standard practice in hotels to tip the housekeeping staff at the conclusion of your stay; this is often between £1 and £2 each day.

Though it's appreciated, tipping should always be determined by the caliber of the work. It's quite OK not to tip if you thought the service was poor or unsatisfactory.

Dining Etiquette

There are a few particular traditions to remember, but overall dining etiquette in Oban is the same as it is throughout the UK. Choosing a table yourself is not usual when eating out;

you wait to be seated. It's courteous to put your napkin on your lap after sitting down and to wait to begin eating until everyone else at the table has been served.

Using cutlery from the outside in—the knife on the right and the fork on the left—is traditional in formal dining situations. To let the server know you're done, place your knife and fork together on your dish, prongs facing up.

It's courteous to hold off on starting to eat until after everyone has been served. When someone passes you a dish, it's polite to accept a little piece rather than helping yourself to a big one.

Thanking the host or server for their hospitality at the end of the dinner is customary, as is offering to assist clear the table or, if dining in someone's house, do the dishes.

Social Norms

Like much of Scotland, Oban has its own particular social norms and conventions that tourists need be aware of in order to have polite conversations with the inhabitants. For instance, it is very appreciated to be on time for appointments, meetings, and social events.

Respect for personal space is also crucial, therefore when talking to someone, keep a comfortable distance. Wait for your turn to speak and pay close attention to what others have to say; interrupting or talking over someone is considered impolite.

Offer to buy a round of drinks for your party in social situations, with each person paying for a round in turn. Known as "getting a round in" this is a typical gesture of friendship and hospitality.

Giving a little present, like a bottle of wine or a bouquet of flowers, to someone you visit is considered courteous. If the host has any other house rules or customs, be sure to take off your shoes when you enter.

Gaining knowledge of these regional manners and traditions will help you to negotiate social situations and respect the beliefs and customs of the Oban residents. Your visit to Oban will be much enhanced by a little consideration and courtesy, whether you're eating out, going to a social event, or just seeing the town.

CHAPTER 13

LEARNING BASIC

SCOTTISH GAELIC

Embracing the language of the country enriches any travel experience by helping you to connect more deeply with the culture and people of a location. Learning basic Scottish Gaelic in Oban, a town with a rich Gaelic tradition, can enhance your experience and establish meaningful contacts with residents.

This chapter offers a complete guide to understanding the fundamentals of the Gaelic language, including vital phrases, language learning tools, and cultural etiquette recommendations.

Essential Gaelic Phrases

Learning a few important Gaelic phrases might help you appreciate the local culture and connect with the people of Oban.

While English is commonly spoken in the area, making an effort to speak Gaelic, even if only for a few words, is highly valued by locals. Here are some key Gaelic phrases to get you started:

Madainn Mhath (MAD-In VAH): Good morning

Feasgar Math (FESH-Kur Mah): Good afternoon/evening

Oidhche Mhath (OY-Khuh VAH): Good night

Tapadh Leat (TAH-Puh Let): Thank you (to one person)

Tapadh Leibh (TAH-Puh Layv): Thank you (to more than one person or in formal settings)

Slàinte Mhath (SLAN-Cha VAH): Cheers/good health

Ciamar A Tha Sibh? (KIM-Ur Uh Ha Shiv): How are you? (formal/plural)

Ciamar A Tha Thu? (KIM-Ur Uh Ha Oo): How are you? (informal/singular)

Is Mise [your name] (Iss MISH-Uh): I am [your name]

Fàilte (FAHL-Tuh): Welcome

Practice these phrases with locals and see how their cheeks light up with gratitude for your efforts to communicate in their language.

Language-Learning Resources

There are several resources available to help you learn Gaelic. Whether you prefer books, online classes, or language exchange programs, there is something for everyone's learning style. Here are some recommended resources to help you along the way:

Books: Boyd Robertson and Iain Taylor's "Teach Yourself Gaelic" provides a thorough approach to learning Gaelic from scratch, including grammar, vocabulary, and pronunciation. "Gaelic for Beginners" written by J. Derrick McClure is another great resource for beginners, with clear explanations and fun exercises to help you learn.

Online Lessons: Websites such as Duolingo and Babbel provide interactive Gaelic lessons that you can complete at your own pace from the comfort of your home. These courses cover everything from fundamental phrases to advanced grammar and conversational abilities, making them suitable for both beginners and intermediate learners.

Language Exchange Programs: Participating in a language exchange program can be a fun and effective method to improve your Gaelic skills while meeting new people. Websites such as ConversationExchange.com pair language learners with native speakers for virtual language exchanges via video chat or messaging, allowing you to practice speaking Gaelic in a helpful and encouraging setting.

Local Classes and Workshops: If you're in Oban for an extended amount of time and want to immerse yourself in the local community, consider taking a Gaelic language class or workshop. Many community centers and cultural groups provide programs for beginners and intermediate learners, offering a structured learning environment as well as opportunity for hands-on experience.

Regardless of which tools you use, consistency and practice are essential for improving your Gaelic language skills. Set aside time each day to study and practice, and don't be afraid to make mistakes—every effort at speaking Gaelic moves you closer to fluency.

Cultural Etiquette Tips

As you learn about Gaelic language and culture, it's crucial to remember cultural etiquette in order to have courteous and meaningful interactions with locals. Here are some etiquette points to bear in mind:

Respect The Language: Gaelic is an important element of Scotland's cultural history, so treat it with respect and care. Avoid making jokes or disparaging remarks about Gaelic, and express appreciation for locals who speak it.

Use Gaelic Greetings: To demonstrate respect for the language and culture, consider greeting locals with Gaelic expressions such as "madainn mhath" (good morning) or "feasgar math" (good afternoon or evening).

Be Open-Minded: Accept the contrasts between Gaelic and your own culture, and approach new experiences with an open mind and a desire to learn. Respect the local norms and traditions, even if they differ from your own.

Get Permission Before Recording or Photographing: If you're at a Gaelic event or dealing with Gaelic speakers, always get permission before recording or photographing them. Respect their privacy and cultural sensitivity, and be aware of any limitations on photography or recording.

By following these cultural etiquette recommendations, you will demonstrate respect for the Gaelic language and culture while also fostering pleasant and lasting interactions with the Oban community.

Language Assistance Services

While English is frequently spoken in Oban, you may occasionally see Gaelic signage or hear Gaelic spoken in public places.

If you require language assistance, there are various services available to help.

Gaelic Language Applications: Install a Gaelic language application on your smartphone for quick and easy translation and pronunciation help on the move. Applications such as "Learn Gaelic" and "Gaelic Dictionary" include comprehensive dictionaries, audio pronunciations, and interactive learning aids to help you explore the language.

Language Hotlines: Some tourist information centers and cultural groups provide language hotlines or helplines, which you can contact or text for translation or interpretation services. Check with your local resources for information on available services and how to get them.

Language Schools And Tutoring Services: If you're staying in Oban for an extended amount of time or want to learn Gaelic, consider enrolling in a language school or hiring a private tutor for personalized language education. Many language schools provide flexible schedules and lesson plans to match your specific learning needs.

Local Community Centers: Oban's community centers and cultural organizations may provide Gaelic language classes, workshops, or conversation groups for students of all skill levels. These programs allow you to practice speaking Gaelic in a supportive and encouraging setting while also connecting with others who share your enthusiasm for the language.

Using these language aid programs will improve your ability to traverse Gaelic-speaking situations and interact with the Oban community.

In summation, studying basic Scottish Gaelic provides opportunities for deeper cultural awareness and genuine connections with Oban residents.

CHAPTER 14

ITINERARIES AND SAMPLE PLANS

Planning a trip to Oban can be both thrilling and daunting, especially with the abundance of things to see and do in this lovely coastal town.

Weekend Getaway

Oban's beautiful beauty and dynamic atmosphere make it ideal for a weekend getaway. With two days to explore, you may see the town's main attractions, eat wonderful food, and take in the breathtaking seaside vistas.

Here's an example agenda for a fantastic weekend away in Oban:

Day One: Arrival and Exploration

Morning: Arrive in Oban and check into your accommodations. Choose a hotel in a central location so you can easily explore the area on foot. Begin the day with a full breakfast from a local café or bakery. To fuel your activities, eat freshly baked pastries, Scottish oatmeal, or a typical full Scottish breakfast.

Mid-Morning: Take a guided walking tour around Oban's medieval town center. Learn about the town's fascinating history, architecture, and landmarks from an expert local guide. See McCaig's Tower, a stunning structure standing atop Battery Hill. Climb the steps to the top for a panoramic view of Oban Bay and its neighboring islands.

Lunchtime: Spend a relaxing lunch at one of Oban's seafood eateries or traditional pubs. Try local favorites like freshly caught seafood, haggis, or substantial stews with a pint of Scottish ale.

Afternoon: Take a guided tour of the Oban Distillery and learn about the whisky-making process. Learn about the distillery's history and manufacturing process, and try a variety of superb single malts. Take a stroll down the scenic esplanade and enjoy views of Oban Bay, which is studded with fishing boats and yachts. Take photographs of the landmark McCaig's Tower standing over the town.

Evening: Enjoy a wonderful evening at a beachfront restaurant that overlooks Oban Bay. Enjoy a delicious seafood feast with locally sourced ingredients and freshly cooked dishes. Wrap off the day with a leisurely stroll down the harborfront promenade, taking in the dazzling lights of the town and the serene serenity of the sea at sunset.

Day Two: Outdoor Adventures and Culinary Delights

Morning: Begin the day with a brisk hike or seaside walk along one of Oban's picturesque pathways. For breathtaking scenery and pure sea air, take the Oban to Dunollie Castle hike or the Ganavan Sands circle. Alternatively, take a guided sea kayaking adventure to discover Oban's craggy coastline and hidden bays. Paddle past steep cliffs, sea caves, and marine creatures while taking in the natural splendor of the area.

Lunchtime: Have a picnic in nature or a light lunch at a coastal café or deli. Sample exquisite sandwiches, locally sourced salads, and handmade desserts to fuel your afternoon travels.

Afternoon: Visit the Scottish SEA creatures Sanctuary to learn about and interact with marine creatures. Explore exhibits featuring seals, otters, sharks, and seahorses, as well as information on regional conservation activities.

Take a picturesque drive or ferry journey to the adjacent Isle of Kerrera to see island life. Explore historic places such as Gylen Castle, meander along isolated beaches, and take in the stunning vistas of Oban and its neighboring islands.

Evening: Return to Oban and have a fantastic meal in a fine-dining restaurant or comfortable cafe. Enjoy gourmet meals made with locally produced ingredients and combined with good wines or craft beers. Wrap up your weekend getaway with a sunset boat around Oban Bay. Relax on deck as you sail past stunning islands, lighthouses, and coastal cliffs, taking in the peace and beauty of the Scottish coast.

Cultural Immersion

A cultural immersion schedule provides guests with a unique opportunity to discover Oban's historical landmarks, museums, and cultural attractions, allowing them to have a better grasp of the town's rich culture and tradition.

Immerse yourself in the local arts, traditions, and cuisine as you discover Oban's lively cultural scene.

Here's an example itinerary for a cultural immersion trip in Oban.

Day One: Heritage And History.

Morning: Begin your cultural immersion by visiting the Dunollie Museum, Castle, and Grounds. Explore the medieval castle ruins, stroll through the picturesque gardens, and visit the museum's displays on Oban's Gaelic roots and maritime history.

Mid-Morning: Participate in a traditional Gaelic language and music workshop at the Dunollie Learning Center. Learn simple Gaelic phrases, practice playing traditional Scottish instruments such as the bagpipes or fiddle, and immerse yourself in Gaelic culture's rich traditions.

Lunchtime: Have a traditional Scottish meal in a local restaurant or pub. Try regional favorites such as cullen skink (smoked haddock chowder), haggis neeps and tatties, or Scotch broth, along with freshly baked bread and a drink of whisky.

Afternoon: Visit the Oban War and Peace Museum to learn about the town's involvement in World War II and contributions to the war effort. Explore exhibits illustrating Oban's maritime heritage, wartime artifacts, and personal stories from local inhabitants.

Evening: Attend a traditional Scottish ceilidh (pronounced "kay-lee") at a nearby venue or community center. Participate in the exciting music and dance as you learn traditional Scottish ceilidh dances such as the Gay Gordons, Strip the Willow, and Dashing White Sergeant.

Day Two: Arts And Culture

Morning: Visit the Rockfield Centre, a lively community arts complex set in a historic old school building. Browse art galleries, participate in workshops and performances, and interact with local artists and craftspeople.

Mid-Morning: Enroll in a traditional Scottish cooking class at a nearby culinary school or community center. Expert chefs will teach you how to make iconic Scottish meals such as haggis, stovies, cranachan, and shortbread.

Lunchtime: Have a leisurely lunch at a classic tearoom or café, sampling homemade soups, sandwiches, and pastries. Enjoy sweet delights such as scones with clotted cream and jam, Victoria sponge cake, and traditional Scottish tablet.

Afternoon: Take a guided tour of the Oban Distillery and sample its products. Learn about the whisky-making process, from malted barley to cask aging, and drink a variety of premium single malts, blends, and limited editions.

Visit the Oban Phoenix Cinema, a magnificent art deco movie theater that dates back to 1935. Watch a classic film or an independent film while taking in the nostalgic atmosphere of this cherished local icon.

Evening: Go to a traditional Scottish music concert or a folk music session at a nearby pub or music venue. Listen to live performances of classic Scottish songs, fiddle tunes, and ballads, and join in the fun as musicians and residents band together to celebrate Scotland's musical history.

In summation: Oban has something for everyone, whether you want a weekend escape full of outdoor adventures and scenic beauty or a cultural immersion experience rich in history, art, and culture. By following these sample itineraries and plans, you'll be able to visit Oban's major sights, experience its culinary pleasures, and immerse yourself in the lively culture and tradition.

Outdoor Adventure

Oban, hidden amongst breathtaking natural landscapes and coastline vistas, is an outdoor enthusiast's dream.

There are plenty of outdoor adventures to be had in and around Oban, ranging from rough hiking paths to thrilling aquatic activities.

Here's a sample itinerary for an exciting outdoor excursion in Oban.

Day One: Exploring the Great Outdoors

Morning: Begin your day with a substantial breakfast at your hotel or one of Oban's quaint cafes. Prepare for a day of outdoor exploring ahead.

Take a morning trek through the nearby Glencruitten Forest, which features old woodlands and lovely pathways. Choose from a variety of difficulty levels, including the Glencruitten Loop and the summit trail to Dunstaffnage Castle for panoramic views of Oban Bay.

Mid-Morning: For thrill seekers, engage on a sea kayaking excursion around Oban's rough shoreline. Join a guided trip or hire kayaks independently to explore sea caves, secluded coves, and coastal cliffs while admiring the breathtaking scenery and marine fauna.

Lunchtime: Have a picnic lunch in nature, or stop at a lovely site overlooking the sea to eat sandwiches, snacks, and local specialties. Take in the fresh air and peacefulness of your surroundings as you prepare for your afternoon adventures.

Afternoon: Head to adjacent Kerrera Island for an afternoon of exploration and outdoor activities. Hike or cycle over the island's picturesque pathways, stopping to admire historic sites such as Gylen Castle and take in panoramic views of Oban and the neighboring islands.

Alternatively, take a guided wildlife-watching cruise to see seals, dolphins, seabirds, and other marine species in their natural environment. Learn about local conservation efforts and marine habitats from qualified guides while experiencing the excitement of wildlife encounters.

Evening: Return to Oban and have a relaxing stroll along the town's gorgeous waterfront promenade. Take in the sunset over Oban Bay and photograph the gorgeous skies reflected in the tranquil waters.

Treat yourself to a great evening at a seafood restaurant or traditional pub, where you can appreciate freshly caught fish and locally produced delicacies coupled with fine wines or craft beer. Reflect on the day's adventures and make plans for further outdoor activities tomorrow.

Day Two: Coastal Excursions and Water-related Thrills

Morning: Get up early and take a wildlife-watching boat cruise to the adjacent islands of Mull, Staffa, or Iona. Keep a watch out for whales, dolphins, puffins, and other marine species as you sail through pristine waterways and visit secluded islands and sea caves.

Mid-Morning: For those who prefer a slower pace, take a beautiful drive along the Argyll Coastal Route to discover hidden beaches, lovely villages, and ancient sites. Stop at viewpoints and photo locations along the trip to capture spectacular coastline views and scenic landscapes.

Lunchtime: Have a seafood lunch in a beachfront restaurant or beachside cafe, sampling freshly caught fish and shellfish cooked in traditional Scottish and foreign methods. For the ideal beach dining experience, pair your meal with a cold white wine or a local craft ale.

Afternoon: Round out your outdoor experiences with an afternoon spent snorkeling or diving in Oban's crystal-clear seas. Diving or snorkeling with expert guides allows you to explore underwater rock formations, kelp forests, and marine animal habitats.

Alternatively, take a sailing tour or boat charter to see Oban's coastal waters from a new angle. Sail by rocky cliffs, secluded islands, and hidden bays while enjoying the excitement of sailing and the peace of the sea.

Evening: Wrap up your outdoor excursion with a sunset boat around Oban Bay, taking in the golden hues of the setting sun and the tranquil serenity of the coastal scenery. Relax on deck with a glass of champagne or whisky, toasting to a day of unforgettable experiences.

Have a goodbye meal at a seaside restaurant, eating your favorite seafood dishes and local specialties while reflecting on your outdoor excursions in Oban. Before leaving this coastal jewel, raise a drink to nature's beauty and the delight of exploring.

Family-Friendly Trip

Oban has a variety of family-friendly attractions and activities to keep people of all ages entertained. Everyone can enjoy activities ranging from wildlife encounters to interactive museums.

Here's an example agenda for a fun family trip to Oban:

Day One: Family Fun and Exploration.

Morning: Begin your day with a visit to the Scottish SEA LIFE Sanctuary, where families can see beautiful aquatic species and learn about conservation initiatives. Explore interactive exhibits, see feeding demonstrations, and get up close and personal with seals, otters, sharks, and other wildlife.

Afterward, take a leisurely stroll around Oban's esplanade, stopping to enjoy the playgrounds and picnic spaces that overlook the bay. Allow the youngsters to burn off some energy while the parents rest and take in the breathtaking scenery.

Mid-Morning: Visit Oban Chocolate Company for a delicious treat and a hands-on chocolate-making workshop. Allow the kids to express their creativity while decorating their own chocolates and indulging in delectable artisanal delicacies.

Lunchtime: Have a family lunch at a local cafe or restaurant, trying kid-friendly options like fish & chips, burgers, or pizza. Choose a location with outside seats to soak up the sun and enjoy al fresco dining.

Afternoon: Spend the afternoon at Oban Bay Play, a wonderful indoor play facility with soft play sections, slides, climbing frames, and interactive activities. Allow the kids to run, jump, and play to their hearts' content while the parents unwind with a cup of coffee at the cafe.

Evening: Take the family out to dinner at a family-friendly restaurant or pub, where you can relax together and sample a range of foods to suit everyone's taste. Finish your day with a leisurely stroll along the harbor front promenade, soaking in the sights and sounds of Oban at night.

Day Two: Nature and Adventure

Morning: Begin your day with Sealife Adventures, where families may go on an exciting wildlife-watching boat excursion in search of seals, dolphins, whales, and seabirds. Learn about the local marine ecosystem and conservation activities from trained guides while having intimate experiences with marine animals.

After the boat excursion, visit Ganavan Sands for a morning of beachcombing, sandcastle building, and seaside activities.

Allow the youngsters to play in the surf, discover rock pools, and enjoy the fresh sea air and beautiful coastal landscape.

Mid-Morning: For families with older children, take a guided sea kayaking tour around Oban's rough shoreline. Paddle past sea cliffs, caves, and hidden coves while learning about marine life and coastal ecosystems from expert guides.

Lunchtime: Have a picnic lunch on the beach or at a lovely viewpoint that overlooks the water. Pack a picnic basket with sandwiches, snacks, and cold beverages, and take a break to refuel and rejuvenate before your afternoon adventures.

Afternoon: Spend the afternoon exploring Dunollie Castle and Grounds, a magnificent castle set on a rock above Oban Bay. Take a guided tour of the castle remains, walk around the picturesque grounds, and admire the panoramic views of the surrounding coastline and islands. Discover the castle's interesting history and the strong Clan MacDougall, who once governed this land.

Evening: Wrap up your family excursion with a guided tour and whisky tasting at Oban Distillery. While adults experience Oban's well-known single malt whisky, children may enjoy non-alcoholic beverages and learn about the whisky-making process from knowledgeable guides.

After the tour, visit a nearby restaurant for a goodbye dinner featuring substantial Scottish cooking and locally produced ingredients. Toast to a memorable family vacation in Oban and share your finest memories and experiences.

Budget Travel

Oban, with its breathtaking natural beauty and rich cultural legacy, provides several options for budget tourists to discover and enjoy without breaking the bank.

Here's a sample plan for exploring Oban on a budget, including reasonable lodging alternatives and free or low-cost activities.

Day One: Exploring Oban on a Budget

Morning: Begin your day with a low-cost breakfast at a local bakery or cafe, where you may eat freshly baked pastries, oatmeal, or a substantial Scottish breakfast without going overboard.

After breakfast, take a self-guided walking tour of Oban's historic town center. Explore the picturesque streets lined with colorful houses, visit the local stores and boutiques, and see sights like as McCaig's Tower and Oban Distillery.

Mid-Morning: Discover the town's maritime heritage and military history at the Oban War and Peace Museum, which is free to explore. Explore exhibits displaying antiques, photographs, and memorabilia from Oban's history, including its participation in World War II and its link to the sea.

Lunchtime: Have a low-cost lunch at a local deli, sandwich shop, or takeaway restaurant, where you may try economical and excellent Scottish staples such as fish and chips, haggis, or a nourishing soup and sandwich combo.

Alternatively, pack a picnic lunch and head to one of Oban's scenic vistas or parks to eat outside while admiring panoramic views of the town and coastline.

Afternoon: Spend the afternoon touring Oban's free or low-cost attractions, including the Oban Distillery Visitor Centre. While the distillery tour has a minor entrance price, it provides an interesting insight into the whisky-making process and concludes with a complimentary sampling of Oban whisky.

Evening: For dinner, choose a neighborhood bar or restaurant that offers low-cost menu alternatives, daily specials, or early bird discounts. While mixing with locals and fellow travelers, indulge in classic pub grub or traditional Scottish cuisine.

After supper, take a leisurely stroll down Oban's waterfront promenade to enjoy the spectacular sunset views over the bay and watch the fishing boats return to the harbor.

Day Two: Outdoor Adventures on a Budget

Morning: Begin your day with a low-cost breakfast at your hotel or a nearby cafe, preparing for a day of outdoor adventures.Pack a picnic lunch and visit one of Oban's gorgeous outdoor attractions, such as Ganavan Sands or Pulpit Hill. Spend the morning hiking, picnicking, or simply resting in the stunning Scottish countryside.

Mid-Morning: Take a guided wildlife-watching boat cruise to see seals, seagulls, and other marine animals in their natural environment. While there is a cost for boat cruises, they are good value for money and deliver spectacular wildlife encounters and scenery.

Lunchtime: Enjoy your picnic lunch at a lovely location overlooking the sea or countryside, soaking up the quiet and beauty of your surroundings. Alternatively, return to Oban and lunch at a low-cost cafe or restaurant serving hearty and reasonable meals.

Afternoon: Spend the day seeing some of Oban's outdoor attractions, including Dunollie Castle and Grounds. While there is a little admission price to visit the castle remains and grounds, it is well worth it for the breathtaking vistas and medieval atmosphere.

Evening: Finish your budget-friendly journey with a casual dinner at a nearby pub or takeaway restaurant, where you can eat good food without breaking the bank. Reflect on your outdoor adventures and memorable experiences in Oban as you choose your next low-cost vacation destination.

Solo Traveler's Guide

Oban is a welcome place for lone travelers, with several options for exploration, leisure, and mingling.

Day One: Solo Exploration and Discovery.

Morning: Begin your day with a solo breakfast at a local cafe or bakery, where you can eat leisurely while organizing your day's activities. Take advantage of the opportunity to people-watch and enjoy the atmosphere of Oban's lively streets.

Mid-Morning: Take a self-guided walking tour of Oban's historic town center, taking in the sights and sounds of this quaint seaside town at your leisure. Visit landmarks such as McCaig's Tower, Oban Distillery, and the Oban War and Peace Museum.

Lunchtime: Have a solo lunch at a quaint cafe or restaurant, enjoying in delectable Scottish food and local delicacies. Choose a window seat or an outdoor table to enjoy views of the busy streets and harbor while dining.

Afternoon: Spend the afternoon seeing Oban's outdoor attractions, including Dunollie Castle and Grounds and the picturesque vistas along the Argyll Coastal Route. Take your time wandering through the gardens, hiking along seaside trails, and photographing the stunning surroundings.

Evening: For dinner, go to a nearby restaurant or pub and enjoy a lone meal while taking in the vibrant ambiance and possibly starting up a conversation with other diners or pleasant locals. Take advantage of the opportunity to meet new people and share your trip experiences.

Day Two: Outdoor Adventure and Relaxation

Morning: Begin the day with an early morning trek or nature walk along one of Oban's picturesque trails or seaside walks. Immerse yourself in the grandeur of Scotland's countryside while enjoying the isolation and tranquility of the natural surroundings.

Mid-Morning: Take a guided wildlife-watching boat excursion around Oban's coastal waterways to see seals, dolphins, seabirds, and other marine life. Accept the opportunity to connect with nature and learn about the local environment from experienced guides.

Lunchtime: Have a solo picnic lunch at a lovely location overlooking the sea or countryside, savoring the solitude and quiet of your surroundings. Before continuing your expedition, take some time to relax, recover, and reflect on your previous outdoor activities.

Afternoon: Spend the day exploring more of Oban's outdoor attractions or practicing solo relaxation and self-care. Enjoy a spa treatment, a yoga class, or a leisurely stroll along the waterfront promenade while admiring the tranquility of the coastal surroundings.

Evening: End your solo excursion with a peaceful meal at a local restaurant or takeaway bistro, relishing the flavors of Scottish cuisine and reflecting on your time in Oban. Raise a glass to your solo travels and the connections you created as you plan your next solo excursion.

Following these sample itineraries and plans allows solitary visitors to appreciate the beauty, charm, and hospitality of Oban while having the freedom and flexibility to explore at their own speed. Oban offers plenty to offer lone visitors seeking adventure, relaxation, or connection.

Romantic Getaways

Oban, with its stunning surroundings, charming seaside ambiance, and romantic allure, is ideal for couples looking for a romantic escape.

From gorgeous walks along the waterfront to intimate dinners overlooking the sea, here's an example itinerary for a romantic getaway to Oban:

Day One: Romantic exploration and discovery.

Morning: Begin your romantic holiday with a leisurely breakfast for two at a cozy cafe or bakery, complete with freshly made pastries, gourmet coffee, and other delectable delicacies. Take your time with each bite and enjoy the lovely aura of the morning.

Mid-Morning: Take a romantic stroll along Oban's waterfront promenade with your spouse. Enjoy the breathtaking views of the bay, breathe in the fresh sea air, and take a moment to enjoy the colorful fishing boats and yachts that line the harbor.

Lunchtime: Have a romantic lunch at a waterfront restaurant or cafe, where you can eat outside on a terrace or balcony overlooking the sea. Enjoy fresh seafood, locally sourced delicacies, and a glass of wine as you celebrate your love and experiences in Oban.

Afternoon: Spend the afternoon discovering Oban's romantic attractions and hidden jewels, such as the peaceful gardens of Dunollie Castle and Grounds and the isolated beaches of Ganavan Sands. Take your time walking hand in hand, pausing to appreciate the natural beauty and historic landmarks along the way.

Evening: For a romantic supper, reserve a seat at a fine dining restaurant or upmarket café renowned for its great cuisine and cozy atmosphere. Enjoy a romantic supper for two, savoring each meal and engaging in meaningful conversation as you celebrate your love and time together in Oban.

Day Two: Romantic Adventures and Relaxation

Morning: Begin your second day by having a romantic breakfast in bed, ordering room service, or making a homemade breakfast for your companion. Enjoy a leisurely meal together, nestled up in the luxury of your accommodations, before embarking on your day's adventures.

Mid-Morning: Take a romantic boat tour of Oban's coastal waterways, where you may discover hidden coves, sea caves, and remote islands with your spouse. A private charter or small group tour will provide a more intimate and personalized experience.

Lunchtime: Have a picnic lunch for two on a private beach or clifftop viewpoint, where you can relish a gourmet buffet of local cheeses, charcuterie, and fresh fruits while taking in the spectacular views of the sea and surroundings.

Afternoon: In the afternoon, indulge in a couples' spa treatment or relaxation session at a local wellness center or luxury resort. Relax together with massages, facials, or aromatherapy treatments to soothe and recharge your bodies and minds.

Evening: Round out your romantic holiday with a private sunset cruise or coastal walk, where you can watch the sun sink below the horizon in a blaze of hues, throwing a beautiful glow over the water and sky. Reflect on your time together in Oban and treasure the memories you've made as you prepare to return home feeling refreshed and renewed.

Couples can enjoy a romantic escape to Oban with this sample itinerary, which includes amazing experiences, cherished moments, and unlimited opportunities for romance and connection. Oban is the ideal setting for a memorable romantic trip, whether you're celebrating a special occasion or simply looking for quality time together.

CHAPTER 15

SAFETY TIPS FOR

VISITORS

Safety is essential when visiting any destination, and Oban is no different. While this picturesque coastal town has a welcoming and friendly environment, tourists must exercise caution to protect their safety and well-being during their stay.

In this chapter, we'll go over general safety considerations, emergency contacts, health and medical facilities, and the value of travel insurance and documentation.

General Safety Precautions

Stay Informed: Before embarking on your trip to Oban, extensively investigate the area to become acquainted with local customs, laws, and any hazards. Keep up with any travel alerts or updates from authoritative sources.

Stay Vigilant: While Oban is typically a safe place, it is critical to exercise caution, particularly in popular tourist areas and during peak tourist seasons. Always keep a watch on your stuff and be alert of your surroundings.

Watch The Weather: Weather in Scotland can be variable, with rain, wind, and fog occurring throughout the year. Check the weather forecast on a frequent basis and prepare for changing conditions by wearing in layers and carrying appropriate gear.

Respect Nature: Oban's natural landscapes are its most appealing feature, yet they can also offer risks if not explored with prudence. When exploring outdoor regions, stick to defined pathways, obey warning signs, and avoid wandering too close to cliff edges or hazardous ground.

Be Hydrated And Nourished: Whether you're hiking, touring, or doing other outdoor activities, it's critical to be hydrated and nourished all day. Bring water and food with you, especially if you plan to spend long periods of time outside.

Use Caution Near Water: Oban's coastline is breathtaking, but it can also be dangerous, with powerful currents and unexpected tides. When swimming, kayaking, or participating in water-based activities, use caution and always obey lifeguard directions and safety rules.

Travel With A Companion: Whenever possible, travel with a companion or in a group, particularly while visiting rural or unknown locations. Having someone with you might add an extra degree of security and support in the event of an emergency.

Follow Local Laws And Customs: Respect the local laws, customs, and cultural sensitivity during your stay to Oban. Familiarize oneself with any applicable rules or restrictions, such as alcohol consumption legislation and designated smoking places.

Emergency Contacts

In the event of an emergency during your stay in Oban, you must have access to necessary contact information for local authorities and emergency agencies.

Here are some crucial figures to keep handy:

Emergency Services (Police, Fire, Ambulance): Call 999

Oban Police Station: +44 (0) 1631 510500.

Oban Hospital: +44 (0) 1631 563491.

Also, if you're staying at a hotel or lodging in Oban, ask about their emergency procedures and contact information for onsite staff or management.

Health And Medical Facilities

Oban has various medical facilities and pharmacies where visitors can obtain medical care if necessary.

These facilities offer a wide range of services, including general healthcare, emergency treatment, and prescription drugs. Some important health and medical facilities in Oban are:

Lorn And Islands Hospital: Situated on the outskirts of Oban, Lorn and Islands Hospital offers a wide range of healthcare services, including accident and emergency treatment, outpatient clinics, and diagnostic services.

Pharmacies: There are several pharmacies in central Oban where visitors can buy over-the-counter medications, prescription drugs, and medical supplies. Pharmacists can also offer advise and guidance on minor medical conditions.

General Practitioners (GPs): Visitors who require non-emergency medical treatment can contact their local GP or healthcare provider. Many GP practices in Oban accept both appointments and walk-ins.

Dentists: If you have a dental emergency, you can go to one of Oban's local dental practices. Dental examinations, emergency dental treatment, and routine operations are all possible services.

Before traveling to Oban, make sure you have comprehensive travel insurance that covers medical emergencies and repatriation. Make sure you understand your insurance policy's coverage limits, exclusions, and emergency contact information.

Travel Insurance And Documents

Travel insurance is a vital part of trip planning since it provides financial security and peace of mind in the event of unforeseen events or emergencies.

When visiting Oban, it is critical to have full travel insurance coverage, which includes:

Medical Coverage: If you become ill or injured while traveling, travel insurance can pay for medical expenditures, hospitalization, and emergency medical evacuation or repatriation.

Travel Cancellation Or Interruption: Travel insurance can compensate you for non-refundable travel expenses in the event of trip cancellation, interruption, or delays caused by insured events such as illness, injury, or natural disasters.

Lost Or Stolen Possessions: Travel insurance can protect you against lost, stolen, or damaged luggage, personal possessions, and travel papers like passports and visas.

Emergency Support Services: Many travel insurance policies provide 24-hour emergency support, which includes access to medical professionals, travel aid, and coordination of emergency medical evacuations.

Before getting travel insurance, carefully read the policy coverage, terms, and conditions to ensure that it suits your unique requirements and provides appropriate protection for your trip to Oban. Keep a copy of your travel insurance policy and emergency contact information on hand at all times during your visit.

In summation, prioritizing safety and preparedness is critical for a pleasurable and worry-free trip to Oban. You may enjoy everything Oban has to offer with confidence and peace of mind if you take general safety precautions, are familiar with emergency contacts and medical services, and have proper travel insurance coverage.

CHAPTER 16

SUSTAINABLE TRAVEL IN

OBAN

Sustainable travel is becoming more essential as we work to reduce our environmental effect while preserving the natural beauty and cultural legacy of places like Oban.

In this chapter, we'll look at eco-friendly lodging options, responsible tourist practices, conservation activities, and community projects that encourage sustainability in Oban.

Environmentally Friendly Accommodation Options

Travelers to Oban can choose eco-friendly accommodations that stress sustainability and environmental responsibility.

These lodgings are dedicated to lowering their carbon footprint, saving resources, and helping local communities. Here are some environmentally friendly hotel choices to consider:

Green Hotels And Lodges: Many Oban hotels and lodges have adopted environmentally friendly practices such as energy-efficient lighting, water conservation measures, and waste reduction programs. Look for lodging that has been accredited by sustainable tourism programs or has acquired eco-friendly certifications.

Eco-Lodges And Eco-Retreats: For travelers looking for a more immersive eco-friendly experience, eco-lodges and eco-retreats provide sustainable lodging in natural locations. These sites frequently use renewable energy sources, encourage biodiversity protection, and provide environmental education programs.

Farm Stays And Rural Retreats: Staying in a farm stay or rural retreat on the outskirts of Oban allows you to gain firsthand experience with sustainable living. These lodgings offer opportunity to practice organic farming, learn about local food production, and support rural communities.

Hostels And Guesthouses: Budget-conscious tourists can find eco-friendly lodging options in Oban. Look for hotels that value sustainability by offering recycling programs, energy-efficient appliances, and locally produced amenities.

Travelers can reduce their environmental effect by staying in Oban's eco-friendly accommodations while also supporting businesses dedicated to sustainability and responsible tourism.

Responsible Tourist Practices

Responsible tourism refers to traveling in a way that supports local people, honors cultural heritage, and reduces negative environmental impacts.

Visitors to Oban can engage in a variety of responsible tourism behaviors that benefit both the place and its inhabitants.

Here are some recommendations for responsible travel to Oban:

Support Local Businesses: When dining out, shopping, or scheduling tours and activities, choose local businesses that benefit the local economy and employ locals. Choose eateries that use locally sourced ingredients, and buy mementos at artisanal shops and craft markets.

Respect Cultural Legacy: Oban has a rich cultural legacy that includes Gaelic traditions, historical sites, and indigenous communities. Respect local customs, traditions, and sacred locations, and look for opportunities to learn about and interact with the local culture through cultural events, festivals, and guided tours.

Minimize Environmental Impact: Practice sustainable behaviors including conserving water and electricity, reducing trash, and adopting eco-friendly transportation. When possible, use walking, cycling, or public transportation, and look for eco-friendly tours and activities that promote conservation and environmental care.

Leave No Trace: When exploring Oban's natural environments, adhere to the Leave No Trace principles by removing any waste, staying on designated pathways, and avoiding damage to vegetation and wildlife habitats. Maintain a safe distance while viewing and photographing wildlife. Avoid disruptive activity.

By adopting responsible tourism habits, visitors may positively contribute to the well-being of Oban's communities and environment while also having meaningful and authentic travel experiences.

Conservation Efforts

Oban is home to a variety of ecosystems, including coastal habitats, marine environments, and protected natural areas, which are the focus of conservation efforts to preserve biodiversity and ecological balance.

Several organizations and activities in Oban are committed to conservation and environmental stewardship:

Marine Conservation: Oban's coastal waters are rich with marine life, including seals, dolphins, and sea birds. Marine conservation organizations safeguard these delicate habitats by doing research, monitoring, and advocating for marine conservation regulations.

Nature Reserves And Protected Areas: Oban is surrounded by breathtaking natural landscapes including as woods, ponds, and mountains that are recognized as nature reserves or conservation areas. These protected areas serve as critical habitat for species while also providing opportunities for outdoor leisure and nature-based tourism.

Wildlife Rehabilitation Centers: In Oban, injured or orphaned wildlife are cared for and rehabilitated at wildlife rehabilitation centers before being released back into the wild. These facilities also serve an important role in teaching the public about wildlife protection and environmental concerns.

Community Conservation Projects: Oban's local communities actively participate in conservation efforts through activities such as beach cleanups, tree planting events, and habitat restoration. These programs engage both residents and visitors in hands-on conservation activities, instilling a sense of environmental care.

Travelers can help to safeguard Oban's natural resources and biodiversity for future generations by volunteering, making donations, or participating in eco-friendly tours and activities.

Community Initiatives

In Oban, community initiatives play an important role in improving sustainability, encouraging community engagement, and empowering residents. These efforts emphasize diverse aspects of community development, environmental protection, and cultural preservation:

Community Gardens And Allotments: Community gardens and allotments allow locals to cultivate their own fruits, vegetables, and flowers, increasing local food production, lowering food miles, and cultivating a sense of community connectedness.

Cultural Festivals And Events: Oban offers a number of cultural festivals and events throughout the year, which celebrate local customs, music, art, and cuisine. These events not only highlight the region's distinct cultural legacy, but also benefit local artists, entertainers, and businesses.

Community-Owned Enterprises: Some Oban businesses and services are locally owned and operated, with earnings reinvested in community projects and initiatives. Supporting community-owned firms positively benefits the community's economic well-being and helps to sustain local livelihoods.

Environmental Education Programs: Oban's environmental education programs and projects seek to create knowledge about environmental issues, encourage sustainable living practices, and empower people to take action to protect the environment. These activities frequently cater to schools, community organizations, and the general public, offering opportunity for hands-on learning and interaction.

Participating in community activities allows visitors to engage with locals, learn about the destination's culture and way of life, and contribute to positive social and environmental change in Oban.

To summarize, sustainable travel in Oban includes a variety of behaviors and projects aiming at reducing environmental effect, helping local communities, and maintaining the destination's natural and cultural legacy. Travelers may make a difference in Oban by staying in eco-friendly accommodations, practicing responsible tourism, supporting conservation efforts, and participating in community initiatives.

CHAPTER 17

PHOTOGRAPHY TIPS

Photography is an excellent method to capture memories and highlight the beauty of Oban's scenery, sites, and culture.

In this chapter, we'll look at photography ideas and techniques to help you take beautiful photographs of Oban.

This chapter will provide you with the knowledge and skills you need to capture fascinating photographs of Oban, from discovering the ideal photo places to mastering lighting and composition, selecting the correct equipment, and enhancing your photos through editing and post-processing.

Best Photo Spots

McCraig's Tower: Perched on a hill overlooking Oban, the tower provides panoramic views of the town, harbor, and neighboring islands. Capture amazing sunrise and sunset photos from this vantage point, with the sun's warm glow illuminating the area.

Oban Bay: The scenic bay of Oban is a popular destination for photographers, with opportunities to capture reflections of boats, colorful buildings along the waterfront, and distant hills beyond. Experiment with different angles and compositions to get unique views of the bay.

Dunollie Castle: Dunollie Castle, which dates back to the 12th century, provides a striking backdrop for photography, especially during golden hour, when the soft light bathes the ruins in a warm glow. Explore the castle grounds to discover unique compositions and perspectives.

Ganavan Sands: This gorgeous beach just outside Oban provides limitless options for beachscape photography, with its golden sands, rocky outcrops, and vistas of the surrounding coastline. To produce dreamy seascapes, photograph reflections in damp sand or use long exposure techniques.

Island Hopping: Take a ferry or boat cruise to the surrounding islands of Mull, Iona, and Staffa, where you'll find rough coasts, historic ruins, and plenty of wildlife. These islands provide several photo options, ranging from stunning sea cliffs to calm beaches and historical landmarks.

Lighting And Composition Tips

Golden Hour: The hours immediately following sunrise and before sunset, known as the golden hour, provide soft, warm light great for photography. Take advantage of this lovely time of day to photograph landscapes in golden hues with lengthy, dramatic shadows.

Rule Of Thirds: The rule of thirds might help you compose visually appealing photos. Divide your frame into thirds, both horizontally and vertically, and place your main subject or focal point at the junction of these lines to create a balanced composition.

Leading Lines: Look for natural or man-made components that can draw the viewer's attention to the landscape, such as highways, paths, or shorelines.

These leading lines give depth and texture to your images while also conveying a sense of movement or direction.

Foreground Interest: Use items in the foreground of your photographs to offer depth and context to the scene. This could range from rocks or flowers in a landscape photo to people or objects in a street setting. Experiment with various foreground elements to make visually appealing compositions.

Experiment With Viewpoints: Don't be scared to try out multiple viewpoints and angles to find the most appealing composition. Get low to the ground for a unique perspective, or climb to a higher vantage point for a more elevated vision. Changing your perspective can radically alter the appearance and feel of your photographs.

Equipment Recommendations

Camera: Whether you use a DSLR, mirrorless camera, or smartphone, select a camera that is appropriate for your skill level and photography goals. While professional-grade cameras provide greater control and image quality, many smartphones now include superior camera technology capable of producing amazing images.

Lenses: Choose lenses that match your photographic style and themes of interest. A versatile zoom lens is perfect for capturing a wide range of scenes, whilst prime lenses provide higher image quality and low-light capabilities. Consider purchasing a wide-angle lens for landscapes and a telephoto lens for animals and close-up photography.

Tripod: A robust tripod is crucial for capturing clear, blur-free photographs, especially in low-light circumstances or with slow shutter speeds. Look for a tripod that is lightweight, compact, and simple to assemble, with adjustable legs and a sturdy mounting plate for your camera.

Filters: Consider purchasing a collection of filters to improve your photographs and generate creative effects in camera. Polarizing filters decrease glare and reflections; neutral density filters enable long exposure photography; and graduated neutral density filters balance exposure in high-contrast subjects.

Accessories: Don't forget to bring additional batteries, memory cards, lens cleaning materials, and a camera bag or backpack to safeguard your equipment while touring Oban.

Editing And Post-Processing Techniques

Adjust Exposure And Contrast: Use editing tools to change the exposure, contrast, and brightness settings in your photographs to improve the overall tonal range and contrast. Adjust the highlights, shadows, and midtones in your photos to bring out details and add depth.

Crop And Straighten: Crop your photographs to improve composition and eliminate distracting things from the frame. Straighten horizons and lines to make your photographs more visually attractive.

Color Enhancement: Adjust the saturation, vibrance, and hue levels in your images to improve their color. Make selective color tweaks to highlight specific colors or create a consistent color palette throughout your photographs.

Sharpen And Reduce Noise: Use sharpening and noise reduction techniques to enhance the clarity and sharpness of your photographs. Masking allows you to selectively sharpen regions of detail while leaving smoother sections of the image alone.

Experiment With Filters And Presets: Use creative filters and presets to give your images artistic effects and stylish styles. To add a distinct aesthetic to your photographs, experiment with black and white conversions, antique film effects, or creative color grading.

By following these photography ideas and techniques, you will be able to create breathtaking photographs of Oban's landscapes, sites, and culture, capturing memories for years to come.

To realize your maximum photographic potential, experiment with varied locations, lighting, and composition, and enjoy the creative process. Oban provides an abundance of opportunity for photography enthusiasts to perfect their abilities and capture the beauty of this quaint seaside town, whether they are seasoned professionals or novices.

CHAPTER 18

INSIDER TIPS FROM

LOCALS

Exploring a place like Oban entails more than just visiting well-known attractions; it's also about discovering hidden jewels, off-the-beaten-path attractions, and local secrets that only insiders are aware of.

In this chapter, we'll give exclusive advice from locals to help you find the true essence of Oban and enjoy it like a local. From hidden jewels and lesser-known sights to insider eating recommendations and local secrets, these suggestions will enrich your Oban experience and allow you to dive deeper into the heart of this picturesque seaside town.

Hidden Gems

Pulpit Hill: Nestled on the outskirts of Oban, Pulpit Hill provides breathtaking panoramic views of the town, harbor, and surrounding landscape. Take a leisurely trek to the summit and enjoy a picnic while admiring the spectacular views.

Gallanach Beach: Escape the throng and explore the tranquil beauty of Gallanach Beach, which is just a short drive from the town center. This hidden gem has immaculate sands, brilliant blue waters, and unobstructed views of the surrounding islands.

Dunstaffnage Castle: Go beyond the well-trodden tourist path to see Dunstaffnage Castle, a medieval fortification steeped in history. Wander around the old ruins, ascend the spiral staircase to the battlements, and experience life centuries ago.

Ganavan Sands Nature Reserve: Nature enthusiasts will enjoy the calm of Ganavan Sands Nature Reserve, which is a refuge for wildlife and birdwatching. Stroll along the beachfront path, look for seagulls and seals, and appreciate the wildflowers in bloom.

Easdale Island: Take a day excursion to Easdale Island, a hidden gem off the coast of Oban that is only accessible by ferry. Explore the small settlement, stop by the fascinating Easdale Island Folk Museum, and take in the raw beauty of this lonely island.

Off-Beaten Path Attractions

Achnabreck Cup And Ring Marks: Learn about ancient history at Achnabreck Cup and Ring Marks, a lesser-known archaeological site in Kilmartin Glen. Admire the prehistoric rock engravings and ponder their strange origins.

Duart Castle: Travel across the Sound of Mull to discover Duart Castle, an enormous fortification built on a rocky headland overlooking the sea. Discover the castle's rich history, admire its medieval architecture, and enjoy panoramic views from the battlements.

Loch Creran Wildlife Reserve: Loch Creran Wildlife Reserve is a hidden jewel located between Loch Creran and the surrounding mountains, where you may immerse yourself in nature. Explore the picturesque pathways, sight otters and eagles, and admire the various flora and animals.

Sgurr Dearg: For ambitious hikers looking for a challenge, try Sgurr Dearg, the tallest peak on the Isle of Lismore. Ascend the difficult slopes, scramble across rocky terrain, and be rewarded with spectacular views of the Inner Hebrides from the peak.

Glen Lonan: Discover the serene beauty of Glen Lonan, a remote glen filled with old trees, gushing streams, and hidden waterfalls. Follow the twisting trails, listen to the sounds of nature, and get away from the hurry and bustle of daily life.

Local Dining Secrets

Cuan Mor: Cuan Mor, a hidden gem in the center of Oban, serves fresh fish and handmade beer. Try the catch of the day, hearty pub favorites, and wash it down with a pint of locally made ale.

Ee-Usk: Enjoy great dining with a view at Ee-usk, a seafood restaurant that overlooks Oban Bay. Enjoy fresh oysters, langoustines, and scallops while admiring magnificent views of the bay and neighboring islands.

George Street Fish Restaurant: Enjoy the flavors of Scotland at George Street Fish Restaurant, a family-run establishment noted for its traditional fish and chips. Enjoy wonderfully crispy batter, delicate fish, and handmade tartar sauce, all with a side of pleasant service.

Waterfront Fishouse Restaurant: The Waterfront Fishouse Restaurant, a hidden gem on the banks of Loch Fyne, allows you to dine like a native. Feast on locally sourced delicacies, such as smoked salmon, mussels, and crab, while admiring the breathtaking waterfront views.

Oban Chocolate Company: Satisfy your sweet craving at the Oban Chocolate Company, a local favorite famed for its handcrafted chocolates and gourmet sweets. Browse the delectable collection of truffles, pralines, and fudge, and purchase a box of chocolates as a tasty souvenir.

Insider Recommendations

Take A Wildlife Tour: A guided wildlife tour provides an up-close look at Oban's plentiful wildlife. Join skilled local guides on boat tours or wildlife safaris to see seals, dolphins, whales, and seabirds in their natural habitats.

Attend A Ceilidh: Immerse yourself in Scottish culture and tradition by attending a ceilidh, which is a lively social gathering with traditional music, dancing, and storytelling. Check local listings for ceilidhs held in pubs, community halls, or cultural institutions.

Explore Local Craft Shops: Help local artisans and craftspeople by exploring Oban's lively craft scene. Browse independent boutiques and galleries for handmade jewelry, pottery, textiles, and artwork, and bring home a one-of-a-kind keepsake of your trip to Oban.

Visit Oban Distillery: Take a guided tour of the distillery to learn about the secrets behind Scotch whisky production. Learn about the whisky-making process, drink a variety of single malts, and take in panoramic views of the town from the distillery's visitor center.

Take A Sunset Sail: Enjoy the magic of Oban's sunsets from the water with a sunset sail around the bay. Relax on deck, sip a glass of champagne, and watch the sky turn pink, orange, and gold as the sun sets.

By following these insider suggestions from locals, you'll discover hidden jewels, visit off-the-beaten-path attractions, dine like a local, and acquire unique insights into Oban's culture and lifestyle.

CHAPTER 19

HISTORICAL AND CULTURAL WALKING TOURS

Exploring Oban on foot is a wonderful opportunity to immerse yourself in its rich history and vibrant culture.

In this chapter, we'll take you on four engaging walking tours of Oban, highlighting its historical landmarks, cultural history, and natural beauty. These walking excursions take you from the picturesque alleys of the city center to the rough shoreline and ancient castles, providing a fascinating peek into Oban's heart and soul.

Oban City Walking Tour

Explore Oban's busy city center, where history meets modernity in a beautiful mix of old and new. This walking tour will guide you around Oban's streets and alleyways, introducing you to historic sites, cultural attractions, and hidden jewels.

McCraig's Tower: Start your walking tour at McCraig's Tower, an iconic monument built atop a hill that overlooks the town and port. Built in the nineteenth century by local banker John Stuart McCraig, the tower provides panoramic views of Oban and the surrounding islands.

Oban Distillery: Take a guided tour of the distillery to learn about the secrets behind Scotch whisky production. Learn about the whisky-making process, from malting and mashing to fermentation and distillation, and then taste a variety of exquisite single malts at the end of the tour.

St. John's Cathedral: Explore St. John's Cathedral, a stunning neo-Gothic church in the center of Oban. Learn about its history and relevance to the local community while admiring its gorgeous stained glass windows, complex brickwork, and serene interior.

Oban War And Peace Museum: Step back in time at the Oban War and Peace Museum, which is housed in a former church from the nineteenth century. Explore exhibitions about Oban's maritime history, wartime experiences, and cultural legacy, which include relics, photographs, and interactive displays.

Dunollie Castle: Wrap up your walking trip with a visit to Dunollie Castle, an ancient fortification built on a rocky promontory overlooking the sea. Explore the castle's ruins, which date back to the 12th century, and enjoy panoramic views of Oban Bay and the surrounding shoreline.

Castle And Clan Tour

Explore Oban's medieval past on a castle and clan tour, which delves into the region's rich history of clan warfare, castle construction, and Highland heritage.

This walking trip, which includes ancient fortresses and picturesque estates, will transport you back to a bygone era of chieftains and warriors.

Dunstaffnage Castle: Start your visit at Dunstaffnage Castle, one of Scotland's oldest stone castles, which is just a short drive from Oban. Built in the 13th century by the MacDougall clan, the castle served as both a strategic fortification and a royal home.

Dunollie Castle: Continue your journey to Dunollie Castle, the ancestral home of the Clan MacDougall. Explore the ruins of this medieval stronghold, positioned on a rocky promontory with a view of the sea, and hear about its turbulent history and aristocratic inhabitants' traditions.

Duart Castle: Cross the Sound of Mull to see Duart Castle, the ancestral home of the Clan Maclean. This magnificent castle, dating back to the 13th century, is steeped in history and tradition, and offers breathtaking views of the surrounding islands and mainland.

Ardchattan Priory: Discover Ardchattan Priory, a historic priory established in the 13th century by the Valliscaulian order. Discover its calm gardens, historic ruins, and stunning stained glass windows, as well as its significance in medieval Scotland's religious and cultural life.

Kilmartin Glen: Wrap up your journey with a visit to Kilmartin Glen, a hallowed region filled with ancient monuments, standing stones, and burial mounds.

Explore the prehistoric sites of Dunadd Fort, Temple Wood Stone Circle, and Nether Largie Standing Stones to learn about Scotland's ancient history.

Whisky Trail Tour

Join a whisky trail tour that showcases Oban's historic whisky producing legacy and the distillers' craftsmanship. From historic distilleries to scenic whisky trails, this walking tour will take you on a trip from grain to glass in the world of Scotch whiskey.

Oban Distillery: Start your whisky trail journey at Oban Distillery, one of Scotland's oldest and most recognizable whisky distilleries. Take a guided tour of the distillery to learn about the whisky-making process, from milling and mashing to fermentation and distillation, and then sample some superb single malts.

Whisky Shop: Visit the whisky shop in Oban's city center, where you'll find a diverse selection of Scotch whiskies, including rare and limited-edition releases. Browse the shelves, speak with expert staff, and purchase a bottle of your favorite whisky to take home as a souvenir.

Coastal Whisky Trail: The coastal whisky route leads around the craggy beaches of Oban Bay, where you'll find magnificent overlooks, hidden coves, and ancient landmarks. Stop along the road to sip a dram of whisky while admiring the stunning seaside views.

Whisky Tasting Experience: Enjoy a whisky tasting in one of Oban's charming pubs or whisky bars. Enjoy a flight of whiskies from various regions of Scotland, experiencing the distinct flavors and smells of each dram while learning about the art of whisky appreciation.

Distillery Tours: Travel beyond Oban to discover other neighboring distilleries on Scotland's whisky path. Visit well-known distilleries on the Isle of Islay, such as Lagavulin, Laphroaig, and Bowmore, or travel to Speyside to explore the legendary whisky distilleries of Glenfiddich, Glenlivet, and Macallan.

Coastal Heritage Tour

Oban's rich maritime history and coastal heritage can be discovered by a walking tour of its gorgeous shoreline, historic harbors, and traditional fishing communities.

This trip emphasizes Oban's deep relationship to the water, including lighthouses, shipwrecks, fishing boats, and seafood markets.

Oban Seaside: Begin your coastal heritage tour on Oban's lovely seaside promenade, which features charming eateries, bustling harbors, and panoramic views of the water. Watch as fishing boats unload their catch for the day and walk along the pier to breathe in the salty sea air.

Dunollie Lighthouse: Explore the Dunollie Lighthouse, a historic beacon set on a rocky outcrop overlooking the entrance to Oban Bay. Built in the nineteenth century to direct ships safely into the harbor, the lighthouse provides breathtaking views of the coastline and adjacent islands.

Oban War Memorial: Pay your respects at the Oban War Memorial, a sad homage to the courageous men and women who have died in conflicts throughout history. Located on

Corran Esplanade, the memorial serves as a somber reminder of the local community's sacrifices.

Ganavan Sands: Take a leisurely stroll along Ganavan Sands, a magnificent stretch of sandy beach located near Oban's town center.

Surrounded by steep cliffs and lush trees, this picturesque beach is ideal for a leisurely beachside walk or a picnic with panoramic views.

Puffin Dive Centre: Visit the Puffin Dive Centre to learn about the region's rich marine life and explore its hidden gems through scuba diving and snorkeling trips. Dive among vibrant coral reefs, explore underwater tunnels, and see intriguing aquatic species in their natural environment.

In summation: These four walking excursions provide a variety of experiences, allowing you to explore Oban's historical sites, cultural legacy, natural beauty, and maritime traditions on foot. Oban's intriguing scenery has something for everyone, whether you prefer castle ruins, whisky distilleries, seaside vistas, or marine experiences.

CHAPTER 20

EXPLORING OBAN'S

LANDMARKS

Oban, with its rich history and breathtaking natural beauty, is home to numerous sites that provide insight into the town's past and present.

From historic castles to modern attractions, each monument reflects Oban's history and cultural significance.

In this chapter, we will look at four prominent landmarks that every visitor to Oban should see.

McCaig's Tower

McCaig's Tower, perched on Battery Hill and overlooking Oban, is one of the town's most distinctive sights. Built in the late nineteenth century by local banker John Stuart McCaig, the tower served as both a memorial to his family and a source of income for local stonemasons during the winter. The edifice, resembling a Roman colosseum, has a series of arches and a central tower that provides panoramic views of Oban Bay and the surrounding islands.

Visitors can ascend the spiral staircase to the summit of the tower, where they will be rewarded with spectacular views over the town, port, and surrounding mountains. The adjacent grounds offer a peaceful respite from the hustle and bustle of the town below, with manicured grass, flower beds, and chairs where visitors may relax and enjoy the view.

McCaig's Tower is especially beautiful at sunset, when the warm colors of the setting sun give a golden glow over the town and bay. It's ideal for photographers, romantics, and anyone looking for a moment of peaceful reflection amidst Oban's breathtaking scenery.

Oban Distillery

No trip to Oban is complete without a tour of Oban Distillery, one of Scotland's oldest and most recognizable whisky distilleries. The distillery, founded in 1794, has been producing quality single malt Scotch whisky for nearly two centuries, utilizing traditional methods and locally sourced ingredients.

Visitors to Oban Distillery can enjoy a guided tour of the facilities and learn about the entire whisky-making process from beginning to end. Every stage of the production process, from milling and mashing to fermentation and distillation, is thoroughly explained, providing insight into the art and science of whiskey creation.

The tour culminates with a tasting session, during which guests can try some of Oban's finest whiskies, including the trademark Oban 14 Year Old single malt. Its rich tastes of honey, citrus, and sea salt perfectly mirror the rugged coastal scenery that surrounds the distillery.

In addition to guided tours, Oban Distillery provides a visitor center and shop where visitors can buy whiskey, souvenirs, and gifts to take home as keepsakes of their trip.

Dunollie Castle

Dunollie Castle, built on a rocky peninsula overlooking Oban Bay, is a medieval fortification steeped in history and folklore. The fortress, which dates back to the 12th century, was formerly the seat of the powerful Clan MacDougall in western Scotland.

Today, Dunollie Castle is in ruins, its aged stone walls bearing witness to centuries of conflict and change. Visitors can visit the castle's remnants, including the magnificent keep, defensive walls, and medieval dwelling quarters, and imagine what life was like for the clansmen who once lived here.

In addition to its historical significance, Dunollie Castle has breathtaking views of Oban Bay and the surrounding shoreline, making it a favorite destination for photographers, hikers, and history buffs alike. A tour to Dunollie Castle provides insight into Scotland's stormy past and the lasting influence of its medieval clans.

Oban War And Peace Museum

The Oban War and Peace Museum, housed in a former church building on Corran Esplanade, is dedicated to preserving memories of Oban's wartime experiences while also promoting modern-day peace and reconciliation. The museum houses a collection of relics, photographs, and papers about Oban's military history, including displays on World War I, World War II, and the local Home Guard.

Visitors to the museum can view displays about the Battle of the Atlantic, the role of women in combat, and the impact of conflict on the local community. Interactive displays and multimedia presentations shed light on the human cost of war and the significance of learning from the past in order to build a more peaceful future.

In addition to its permanent exhibitions, the Oban War and Peace Museum hosts temporary displays, educational programs, and community events all year. It's a place where people of all ages may learn, reflect, and connect with history in meaningful ways.

These four landmarks provide an insight into Oban's rich heritage, ranging from ancient history to present cultural attractions. Oban's prominent sites provide something for everyone, whether you're looking to explore old castles, sample exquisite whisky, or learn about the town's military history.

CHAPTER 21

ACCOMMODATION AND DINING DIRECTORIES

Finding the ideal spot to stay and eat is essential for a memorable vacation to Oban.

In this chapter, we'll present extensive directories of popular lodgings, restaurants, cafés, pubs, clubs, and attractions to help you organize your trip effectively.

Addresses And Locations Of Popular Accommodation

Oban Bay Hotel And Spa

Address: Corran Esplanade, Oban, Argyll, PA34 5AE

This beachfront hotel offers exquisite suites with spa amenities and spectacular views of Oban Bay.

Perle Oban Hotel

Address: Station Square in Oban, Argyll, PA34 5RT,

This hotel has modern accommodations, a restaurant, and a cocktail lounge.

The Regent Hotel

Address: Corran Esplanade, Oban, Argyll, PA34 5PZ

The Regent Hotel is a family-run hotel facing the bay with pleasant accommodations, a restaurant serving Scottish cuisine, and a cozy bar.

Columba Hotel

Address: North Pier, Oban, Argyll, PA34 5QD.

Located near the ferry terminal, this historic hotel has exquisite rooms, a restaurant, and a lounge with panoramic views of the bay.

Lagganbeg Guesthouse

Address: Gallanach Road, Oban, Argyll, PA34 4EG - A beautiful guesthouse overlooking the port with pleasant accommodations and a friendly Scottish welcome.

Addresses And Locations Of Popular Restaurants And Cafés

EE-Usk

Address: Gallanach Road, Oban, Argyll, PA34 4LS

A seafood restaurant set on the waterfront, noted for its fresh seafood meals and breathtaking views of the bay.

Coast Restaurant

Address: George Street, Oban, Argyll, PA34 5RX.

This is a trendy restaurant that serves locally sourced fish and Scottish cuisine.

Cuan Mor

Address: George Street, Oban, Argyll, PA34 5NX.

A vibrant gastropub with a broad menu including pub classics, craft brews, and live music events.

Piazza

Address: Stafford Street, Oban, Argyll, PA34 5NJ

An Italian restaurant and café offering wood-fired pizzas, pasta dishes, and gelato in a calm setting.

Oban Chocolate Company

Address: Corran Esplanade, Oban, Argyll, PA34 5PS.

This is a beautiful café and chocolatier that serves handmade chocolates, pastries, and hot drinks with views of the bay.

Addresses And Locations Of Popular Bars And Clubs

Markie Dans

Address: Located at 2 Victoria Crescent in Oban, Argyll, PA34 5DX,

This is a charming Scottish bar offering a variety of whiskies, ales, and pub food.

The Lorne Bar

Address: Located at Stevenson Street in Oban, Argyll (PA34 5NA).

A welcoming neighborhood bar known for live music, quiz nights, and a diverse drink menu.

Cuan Mor Bar

Address: Located on George Street in Oban, Argyll, PA34 5NX,

Cuan mor bar serves craft beers, cocktails, and spirits.

Corran Halls

Address: Located at Corran Esplanade in Oban, Argyll, PA34 5AB.

Curran halls is a multi-purpose venue that hosts live music, comedy shows, and club nights with views of Oban Bay.

Lorne Bar

Address: Located in Stevenson Street in Oban, Argyll (PA34 5NA).

A classic Scottish bar with a casual environment that serves whiskey, beers, and substantial pub fare.

Addresses and Locations Of Major Attractions

Oban Distillery

Address: Stafford Street, Oban, Argyll, PA34 5NH.

Enjoy a guided tour of the distillery, learn about the whisky-making process, and enjoy a range of exquisite single malts.

Dunollie Stronghold

Address: Dunollie Road, Oban, Argyll, PA34 5TT)

Dunollie stronghold offers panoramic views of Oban Bay and the surrounding shoreline as visitors explore the ruins of this ancient stronghold.

McCaig's Tower

Address: Battery Hill, Oban, Argyll, PA34 5DP.

Climb to the summit of this iconic monument to enjoy panoramic views over Oban Bay, the town, and the surrounding islands.

Oban War And Peace Museum

Address: Located at Corran Esplanade in Oban, Argyll (PA34 5PX). Learn about Oban's wartime experiences and the local community's attempts to promote peace and healing.

Oban Sea Life Sanctuary

Address: Dunollie Road, Oban, Argyll, PA34 5TT.

The Oban Sea Life Sanctuary allows you to watch seals, otters, sharks, and other amazing wildlife up close.

McCaig's Tower

Address: Battery Hill, Oban, Argyll, PA34 5DP.

This renowned landmark offers panoramic views of Oban Bay, the town, and the surrounding islands.

Oban Chocolate Company

Address: Corran Esplanade, Oban, Argyll, PA34 5PS.

Enjoy your sweet tooth at this beautiful café and chocolatier, which serves handmade chocolates, pastries, and hot beverages.

Ganavan Sands

Address: Ganavan Road, Oban, Argyll, PA34 5TU.

Enjoy a leisurely stroll or picnic on this gorgeous sandy beach, which offers breathtaking views of the coastline and adjacent islands.

Dunstaffnage Castle And Chapel

Address: Dunbeg, Oban, Argyll, PA37 1PZ.

Visit the ruins of this medieval castle, which dates back to the 13th century, and the surrounding chapel, one of Scotland's oldest stone constructions.

Oban Phoenix Cinema

Address: George Street, Oban, Argyll, PA34 5NX.

For a one-of-a-kind cinematic experience, visit this lovely independent cinema located in a former church.

These top sites provide a varied range of experiences, including historic landmarks, natural marvels, cultural venues, and culinary pleasures.

CHAPTER 22

CONCLUSION

As your stay in Oban comes to an end, it's time to reflect on the memorable experiences you've had, appreciate the memories you've created, and say goodbye to this charming seaside town.

In this final chapter, we'll reflect on your Oban trip, look at some farewell rituals, talk about your future adventure, and depart Oban with memories to treasure.

Reflecting On Your Oban Experience

As you prepare to leave Oban, take a minute to think on the many experiences you've had here. Perhaps you've seen historic castles, enjoyed wonderful seafood, gone on outdoor excursions, or simply admired the gorgeous countryside. Consider the memories that have stayed with you, the sights and sounds that have moved you, and the ties you've formed with the people and places of Oban.

Oban has surely left an impression on you, from its rocky shoreline to its locals' friendly hospitality. Whether you spend a few days or a few weeks exploring its wonders, the experiences you made here will last long after you leave.

Farewell Traditions In Oban

In Oban, saying goodbye is frequently accompanied with time-honored traditions reflecting the town's rich history and legacy. One such custom is the lighting of the "Farewell Fire," which is a symbolic gesture of saying goodbye to visitors and wishing them safe journeys back home.

This ritual is commonly carried out on the shores of Oban Bay, where locals and visitors come to watch the flames dance against the backdrop of the setting sun.

Another farewell ritual in Oban is to share "Drambuie," a traditional Scottish beverage made from whiskey, honey, herbs, and spices. This sweet and aromatic beverage is frequently served as a show of hospitality and kindness, representing friendship and camaraderie. Sharing a toast with newfound friends or fellow tourists is an appropriate way to conclude your time in Oban and commemorate the memories you've created together.

Plan Your Next Adventure

As you say goodbye to Oban, it's normal to begin thinking about your next trip. Whether you're returning home or going on another journey, take some time to reflect on what you've learned and experienced while in Oban.

Perhaps you've discovered a new love of outdoor adventure, a taste for Scottish cuisine, or a drive to learn more about Scotland's rich history and culture.

Use your time in Oban to plan your next trip, whether it's exploring other coastal communities along Scotland's west coast, venturing further into the country's highlands and islands, or beginning on a new adventure in a far-flung location. Allow the experiences you created in Oban to feed your wanderlust and guide you on your next adventure.

Leave Oban With Memories To Cherish

As you depart Oban, take a moment to reflect on the memories you've made here.

Remember the laughs you had with friends, the excursions you went on, and the peaceful moments you spent admiring the beauty of Oban's natural surroundings. As you continue your journey, keep these memories in mind as a reminder of the kindness and generosity you received in this coastal refuge.

As you say goodbye to Oban, remember that you're departing with more than just memories; you're taking a portion of its soul, beauty, and charm. Until we meet again, may your journeys be full with adventure, discovery, and the excitement of new experiences.

As you conclude your stay in Oban, may the memories you've created here continue to inspire and enrich your life's journey. Farewell, Oban, until we meet again.

APPENDIX

USEFUL RESOURCES

This appendix contains a number of useful resources to help you make the most of your trip to Oban.

These resources, which include emergency contact information, maps and navigational tools, further reading and references, and important local words, can assist ensure a smooth and pleasurable visit.

Emergency Contacts

Emergency Services: Dial 999 if you need police, fire, or medical assistance.

Oban Police Station

Address: Albany Street, Oban, Argyll, PA34 4AR.

Phone: 101 (non-emergency)

Oban Hospital

Address: Glengallan Road, Oban, Argyll, PA34 4HH.

Phone: +44 (0) 1631 567500

Coastguard

Phone: 999 or 112

Mountain Rescue

Phone: 999 or 112

Maps And Navigational Tools

Websites

Google Maps

Website: www.maps.google.com

Description: Provides detailed maps, satellite imagery, and street views. Offers route planning for traveling by foot, car, bicycle, or public transportation.

OpenStreetMap

Website: www.openstreetmap.org

Description: A free, editable map of the world that allows users to view and edit geographical data. Great for detailed local maps.

Here WeGo

Website: www.wego.here.com

Description: Offers maps, driving directions, and public transit information. Useful for finding routes and exploring different modes of transport.

ViaMichelin

Website: www.viamichelin.com

Description: Provides maps, route planning, traffic updates, and travel guides. Ideal for planning trips and getting real-time traffic information.

VisitScotland

Website: www.visitscotland.com

Description: Official tourism website for Scotland, offering comprehensive travel information, maps, and guides for various destinations, including Oban.

Apps

Google Maps

Available on: Android, iOS

Website: www.maps.google.com

Description: Offers turn-by-turn navigation, real-time traffic updates, local business information, and offline maps.

MAPS.ME

Available on: Android, iOS

Website: www.maps.me

Description: Offline maps with turn-by-turn navigation. Useful for navigating without an internet connection.

Citymapper

Available on: Android, iOS

Website: www.citymapper.com

Description: Provides detailed public transit information, real-time departures, and route planning for walking, cycling, and public transportation.

Here WeGo

Available on: Android, iOS

Website: www.wego.here.com

Description: Offline maps, turn-by-turn navigation, and detailed public transit information.

Waze

Available on: Android, iOS

Website: www.waze.com

Description: Community-driven traffic and navigation app. Provides real-time traffic updates and alerts about road conditions, accidents, and police traps.

Komoot

Available on: Android, iOS

Website: www.komoot.com

Description: Ideal for outdoor activities like hiking and biking. Provides route planning and navigation for outdoor adventures.

Public Transport Apps

Traveline Scotland

Available on: Android, iOS

Website: www.travelinescotland.com

Description: Offers comprehensive public transport information for Scotland, including bus, train, and ferry schedules and route planning.

ScotRail

Available on: Android, iOS

Website: www.scotrail.co.uk

Description: Official app for Scotland's national railway. Provides train schedules, ticket booking, and real-time updates for trains in and around Oban.

CalMac Ferries

Available on: Android, iOS

Website: www.calmac.co.uk

Description: Official app for Caledonian MacBrayne ferries, offering schedules, ticket booking, and real-time updates for ferry services connecting Oban to various islands.

Additional Tools

Rome2Rio

Website: www.rome2rio.com

Available on: Android, iOS

Description: Global travel planning platform that provides detailed information on how to get from one place to another using various modes of transport, including flights, trains, buses, ferries, and cars.

TripAdvisor

Website: www.tripadvisor.com

Available on: Android, iOS

Description: Offers reviews and recommendations for hotels, restaurants, and attractions. Useful for planning trips and finding points of interest in Oban.

Local Resources

Oban Tourism

Website: www.oban.org.uk

Description: Provides comprehensive information about attractions, events, accommodations, and maps of Oban.

Explore Oban

Website: www.exploreoban.com

Description: Offers detailed information on activities, dining, shopping, and accommodations in Oban.

Oban Town Map: Obtain a physical copy of the Oban town map from the local tourist information center or hotels. It gives a full description of the town's layout, including major attractions and areas of interest.

Map of Oban, Scotland

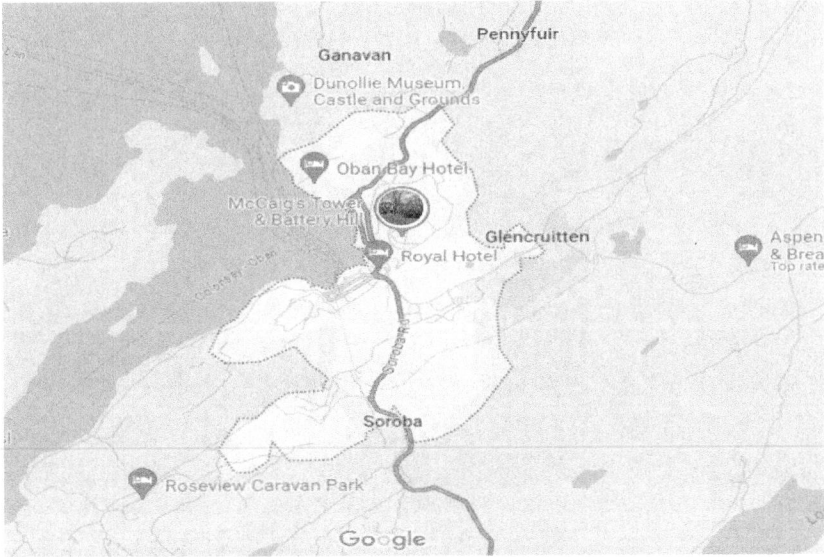

https://maps.app.goo.gl/D2LQo5VzkE8PCqDg6

How to Scan a QR Code:

- Open your device's camera

- Point it at the QR code

- Tap on the notification

- Follow the link to access the content

Map of Hotels in Oban, Scotland

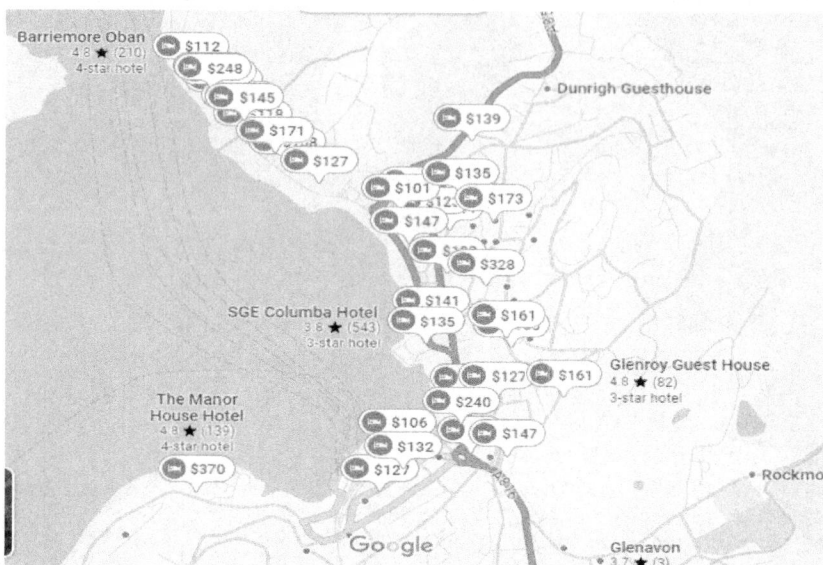

https://maps.app.goo.gl/3WqvdPPMKHt9QThY9

How to Scan a QR Code:

- Open your device's camera

- Point it at the QR code

- Tap on the notification

- Follow the link to access the content

Map of Attractions in Oban Scotland

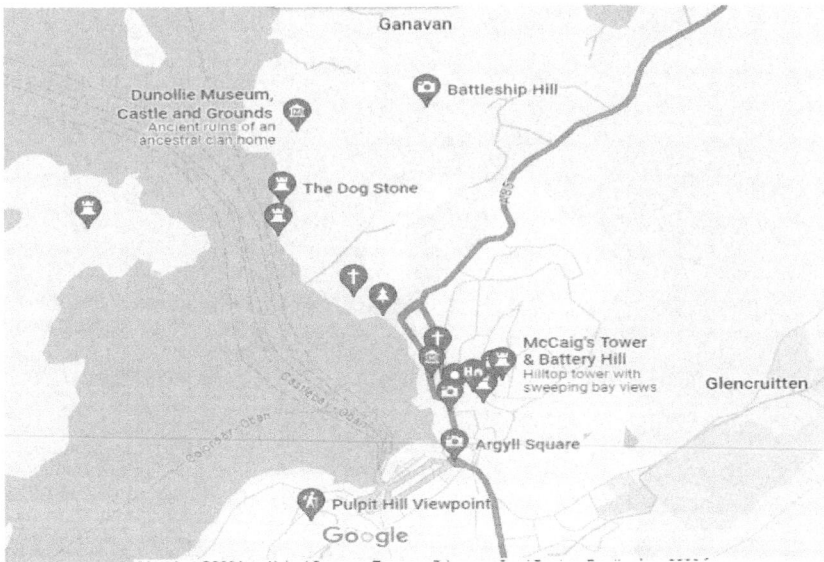

https://maps.app.goo.gl/kJAZrPjn32WJqr3m7

How to Scan a QR Code:

- Open your device's camera

- Point it at the QR code

- Tap on the notification

- Follow the link to access the content

Map of Resturants in Oban Scotland

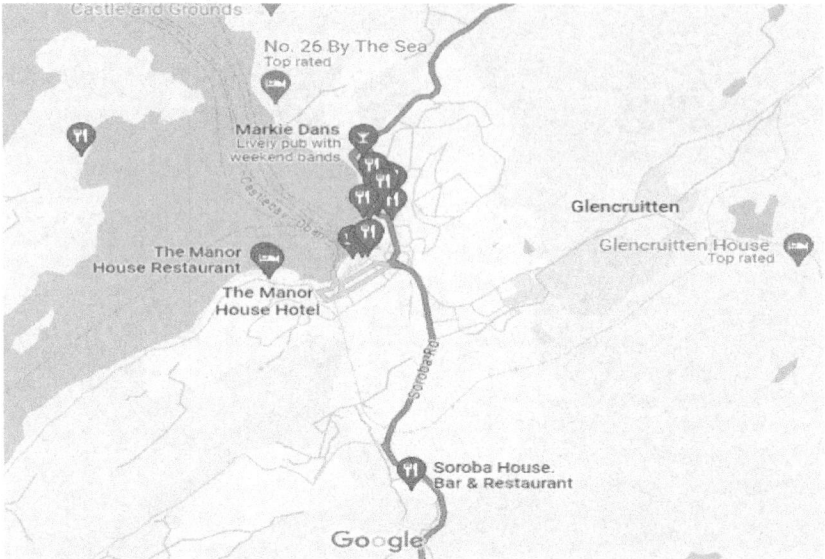

https://maps.app.goo.gl/amqtoByozzZ8Cp8j8

How to Scan a QR Code:

- Open your device's camera
- Point it at the QR code
- Tap on the notification
- Follow the link to access the content

Additional Reading And References

Oban Tourist Information Center (www.oban.org.uk): The official website provides comprehensive information on attractions, events, and lodgings.

VisitScotland (www.visitscotland.com): VisitScotland's website Offers travel guides, itineraries, and ideas for experiencing Scotland, including Oban.

Lonely Planet Scotland

(www.lonelyplanet.com/scotland):

The Lonely Planet Scotland guidebook provides thorough information on Oban, including recommendations for lodging, restaurants, activities, and more.

Historic Environment Scotland

(www.historicenvironment.scot): Discover Scotland's rich history and heritage, including landmarks around Oban.

Useful Local Phrases

"Slàinte Mhath!" (Slan-Ge-Var): Cheers! (Literally translates to "good health!")

"Ciamar A Tha Sibh?" (Kee-Mar A Ha Shee-v): How are you?

"Tapadh Eibh" (Ta-Pa Layv): Thank you (formal).

"Feasgar Math" (Fes-Ker Mah): Good afternoon.

"Fàilte Gu Oban" (Fal-Che Gue Oh-Ban): Welcome to Oban.

"Ceud Mìle Fàilte" (K-Yu-Mee-Le Fal-Che): A hundred thousand welcomes.

Remember to use these phrases to welcome locals and express your gratitude for their hospitality throughout your trip to Oban.

Addresses And Locations Of Popular Accommodation

The Royal Hotel Oban

Address: Argyll Square, Oban, Argyll, PA34 4BE.

Website: www.royalhotel-oban.com

The Regent Hotel

Address: Corran Esplanade, Oban, Argyll, PA34 5PZ.

Website: www.regenthoteloban.co.uk

Columba Hotel

Address: North Pier, Oban, Argyll, PA34 5QD.

Website: www.columbahoteloban.co.uk

Oban Bay Hotel

Address: Corran Esplanade, Oban, Argyll, PA34 5AE.

Website: www.crerarhotels.com/oban-bay-hotel

The Ranald Hotel

Address: 41 Stevenson Street, Oban, Argyll, PA34 5NA.

Website: www.theranaldhotel.com

Addresses And Locations Of Popular Restaurants And Cafés

EE-Usk

Address: North Pier, Oban, Argyll, PA34 5QD.

Website: www.eeusk.com

Café Spice

Address: 10 Argyll Square, Oban, Argyll, PA34 4AZ.

Website: www.cafespiceoban.co.uk

Piazza Italian Restaurant

Address: 4 Stafford Street, Oban, Argyll, PA34 5NJ.

Website: www.piazzaitalianrestaurant.co.uk

Cuan Mor

Address: 55 George Street, Oban, Argyll, PA34 5DS.

Website: www.cuanmor.co.uk

Oban Chocolate Company Café

Address: Corran Esplanade, Oban, Argyll, PA34 5PS.

Website: www.obanchocolate.co.uk

Addresses And Locations Of Popular Bars And Clubs

The Oban Inn

Address: 22 Stafford Street, Oban, Argyll, PA34 5NJ.

Website: www.obaninn.com

Markie Dans

Address: 2 Craigard Road, Oban, Argyll, PA34 5NP.

Website: www.markiedans.com

Aulay's Bar

Address: 8 Airds Crescent, Oban, Argyll, PA34 5SQ.

Website: www.aulays.com

The Lorne Bar

Address: 57 George Street, Oban, Argyll, PA34 5DS.

Website: www.lorneoban.co.uk

Corryvreckan Whisky Bar

Address: 1 Stafford Street, Oban, Argyll, PA34 5NH.

Website: www.corryvreckanwhisky.com

Addresses And Locations Of Top Attractions

McCaig's Tower

Address: Battery Hill, Oban, Argyll, PA34 5DP.

Oban Distillery

Address: Stafford Street, Oban, Argyll, PA34 5NH

Website: www.obanwhisky.com

Dunollie Castle

Address: Dunollie Road, Oban, Argyll, PA34 5TT.

Website: www.dunollie.org

Oban War and Peace Museum

Address: Corran Esplanade, Oban, Argyll, PA34 5PX.

Website: www.obantown.org.uk/museum

Ganavan Sands

Address: Ganavan Road, Oban, Argyll, PA34 5TU.

Image Attributions

Printed in Dunstable, United Kingdom